Understanding Bean Validation 2.0

Bean Validation

Antonio Goncalves

2021-05-03

Table of Contents

Understanding Bean Validation 2.0

The distribution of the book is made through Amazon KDP (Kindle Direct Publishing).[1]

Any source code referenced by the author in this text is available to readers at https://github.com/agoncal/agoncal-fascicle-bean-validation/tree/2.0. This source code is available for reproduction and distribution as it uses an MIT licence.[2]

- www.antoniogoncalves.org
- agoncal.teachable.com
- www.amazon.com/author/agoncal

You can find two different formats of this fascicle:

- eBook (PDF/EPUB): https://agoncal.teachable.com/p/ebook-understanding-bean-validation
- Paper book: http://amazon.com/Understanding-Bean-Validation-2-0-fascicle/dp/1980399026 (ISBN: 9781980399025)

Version Date: 2021-05-03

To my wonderful kids, Eloise, Ligia and Ennio, who are the best thing life has given me.

Foreword

Exactly nine years ago, I received an email which would fundamentally change my professional life fundamentally.

The sender was Emmanuel Bernard, spec lead of Bean Validation at that time, asking me whether I'd be interested in writing the documentation for the Bean Validation reference implementation. I had published a few blog posts on Bean Validation and apparently Emmanuel liked them, so he offered me this job. I felt honoured ("Wow, they read my blog?!"), excited ("Yeah, I'll become a famous open source contributor!") but also a bit scared ("Hmm, can I even do that?"). Without thinking too long, I accepted the challenge and went off to write the first chapters of the Hibernate Validator reference documentation. After a while, I sent in a patch file which was eventually committed to the SVN repository. Boy, was I proud?!

I had no idea that this would be the first step on my path to working full-time on open source and even becoming the Bean Validation spec lead myself one day. But I had learned an important thing: thorough documentation, written in an easy-to-follow style is a vital factor for software to become successful. The challenge lies in hitting the sweet spot of completeness (all the relevant features should be covered) and conciseness (the reader should be able to quickly find the information they're after). The best functionality isn't worth much if potential users cannot easily find out about it.

That's why I was immediately convinced of Antonio's idea of ripping apart his tremendously successful book on Java EE and extracting multiple, smaller fascicles out of it. Each one focuses on one specific API, providing a gentle introduction to it as well as discussing more advanced topics at the same time. It's with great joy that I see that the first of these fascicles is dedicated to Bean Validation.

Based on his extensive experience of using Bean Validation in many Java EE and Spring based projects, Antonio did an outstanding job writing this fascicle. Starting with the basics of putting data validation into the wider context of application development and of setting up your first Bean Validation application, the fascicle touches all the important aspects of Bean Validation such as using built-in and custom constraints, message interpolation, validation groups, method validation and much more. A wide range of examples shows, in depth, how to use the API, and there's even detailed instructions for setting up your development environment, making it very easy to get started.

Since I received that email from Emmanuel in February 2009, Bean Validation has come a long way. Closely integrated with many other specifications and technologies such as JPA, JAX-RS, CDI, JavaFX or Spring, it's successfully used in countless projects. Bean Validation 1.1 added the notion of method validation, making it trivial to automatically validate parameters and return values upon method invocation. Bean Validation 2.0, released in 2017 and part of Java EE 8, brought closer integration with Java 8 and the long-awaited support for validating the elements of any generic container type. How this is done? Find out about this and much more by turning over and diving into this excellent fascicle!

Gunnar Morling
Spec Lead of Bean Validation 2.0 (JSR 380)

Hamburg, February 2018

[1] KDP https://kdp.amazon.com

[2] MIT licence https://opensource.org/licenses/MIT

About the Author

Antonio Goncalves is a senior software architect living in Paris. Having been focused on Java development since the late 1990s, his career has taken him to many different countries and companies where he now works as a recognised consultant. As a former employee of BEA Systems (acquired by Oracle), he developed a very early expertise on distributed systems. He is particularly fond of open source and is a member of the OSSGTP (Open Source Solution Get Together Paris). Antonio loves to create bonds with the community. So, he created the Paris Java User Group in 2008 and co-created Devoxx France in 2012 and Voxxed Microservices in 2018.[3]

Antonio wrote his first book on Java EE 5, in French, in 2007. He then joined the JCP to become an Expert Member of various JSRs (Java EE 8, Java EE 7, Java EE 6, CDI 2.0, JPA 2.0, and EJB 3.1) and wrote *Beginning Java EE 7* and *Beginning Java EE 8* with Apress.[4] Still hooked on sharing his knowledge, Antonio Goncalves decided to then self-publish his later fascicles.

For the last few years, Antonio has given talks at international conferences, mainly on Java, distributed systems and microservices, including JavaOne, Devoxx, GeeCon, The Server Side Symposium, Jazoon, and many Java User Groups. He has also written numerous technical papers and articles for IT websites (DevX) and IT magazines (Java Magazine, Programmez, Linux Magazine). Since 2009, he has been part of the French Java podcast called Les Cast Codeurs.[5]

In recognition of his expertise and all of his work for the Java community, Antonio has been elected **Java Champion**.[6]

Antonio is a graduate of the Conservatoire National des Arts et Métiers in Paris (with an engineering degree in IT), Brighton University (with an MSc in object-oriented design), Universidad del Pais Vasco in Spain, and UFSCar University in Brazil (MPhil in Distributed Systems). He also taught for more than 10 years at the Conservatoire National des Arts et Métiers where he previously studied.

Follow Antonio on Twitter (@agoncal) and on his blog (www.antoniogoncalves.org).

[3] Devoxx France https://devoxx.fr

[4] Amazon https://www.amazon.com/author/agoncal

[5] Les Cast Codeurs https://lescastcodeurs.com

[6] Java Champions https://developer.oracle.com/javachampions

Acknowledgments

In your hands, you have a technical fascicle that comes from my history of writing, learning and sharing. When writing, you need a dose of curiosity, a glimpse of discipline, an inch of concentration, and a huge amount of craziness. And of course, you need to be surrounded by people who help you in any possible way (so you don't get totally crazy). And this is the space to thank them.

First of all, I really want to thank my proofreading team. After the process of writing, I was constantly in contact with Gunnar, Youness, and Guillaume who reviewed the book and gave me precious advice. I have to say, it was a real pleasure to work with such knowledgeable developers.

It is a great honour to have **Gunnar Morling** write the foreword for this fascicle. Gunnar is the Specification Lead for Bean Validation 2.0 (JSR 380) and works as a Principal Software Engineer for Red Hat. An open source enthusiast by heart, he contributes to projects such as Hibernate Validator, Search, ORM and OGM and is the lead of Debezium, a platform for change data capture. He is also the founder of MapStruct, a code generator for bean mappings. Gunnar has spoken at conferences such as Devoxx, JavaOne, JavaZone and many others. He tweets as @gunnarmorling and occasionally blogs at http://in.relation.to/gunnar-morling. Gunnar lives and works in Hamburg, Germany.[7]

Youness Teimouri is a Senior Software Java Developer with over a decade of experience in Java development. He has utilised Java stack to grow numerous companies in a variety of industries such as Telecoms, ERP systems and Mobile Banking. He has co-authored and contributed to some papers on Cloud-Computing and some of my previous books. Youness is fascinated by the endless possibilities of Java in different industries and enjoys mentoring junior developers, inspiring them to develop their own Java skill-set. He lives in Canada.[8]

Guillaume Smet is a Senior Software Engineer at Red Hat. He works primarily on Hibernate Validator, Hibernate Search and Hibernate OGM. An Open Source contributor since 2001, he has contributed to a lot of Open Source software (PostgreSQL, pgFouine, GForge etc.). In his spare time, he plays volleyball, does yoga and enjoys a good book - preferably from John Irving. Guillaume blogs about Hibernate at http://in.relation.to/guillaume-smet. He lives in Lyon, France.[9]

Thanks to my proofreader, **Gary Branigan**, who added a Shakespearean touch to the fascicle.

I could not have written this fascicle without the help and support of the Java community: blogs, articles, mailing lists, forums, tweets etc.

The fascicle you have in your hands uses a rich Asciidoctor 2.0.14 toolchain, making it possible to create PDF, EPUB and MOBI files. I am really grateful to the entire Asciidoctor community, and to Dan Allen and Marat Radchenko in particular, who helped me in sorting out a few things so that the end result looks so great.[10] PlantUML is an amazing tool with a very rich syntax for drawing diagrams... and sometimes, you need a bit of help. So, thanks to the PlantUML community.[11] As for the text editor used to write this fascicle, you might have guessed: it's an IDE! Thank you JetBrains for providing me with a free licence for your excellent IntelliJ IDEA.[12]

Living in Paris, I also have to thank all the bars who have given me shelter so that I could write while drinking coffee and talking to people: La Fontaine, Le Chat Bossu, La Grille, La Liberté and

Bottle Shop.

As you might have guessed, I have a passion for IT. But I have other passions such as science, art, philosophy, cooking... and music (I even play jazz guitar). I cannot work without listening to music, so while I was writing this fascicle, I spent most of my time listing to the best radio ever: FIP.[13] Thank you FIP.

And a big kiss to my wonderful kids, Eloise, Ligia and Ennio. They are the best present life has given me.

Thank you all!

[7] Gunnar Morling http://in.relation.to/gunnar-morling

[8] Youness Teimouri http://www.youness-teimouri.com

[9] Guillaume Smet http://in.relation.to/guillaume-smet

[10] Asciidoctor http://asciidoctor.org

[11] PlantUML http://plantuml.com

[12] IntelliJ IDEA https://www.jetbrains.com/idea

[13] FIP https://www.fip.fr

Introduction

In the late 90s, I was working on J2EE 1.2: the very first release of the *Java Enterprise Edition*. It was also the time where companies started to realise the potential of the Internet for their business. For a few months, I worked for a famous English airline company setting up their e-commerce website. Yes, it was a time where you would usually buy a flight or train ticket at a travel agency. This revolutionary move (buying flights online) came at a technical cost: a cluster for static content (HTML, CSS, images), a cluster for the web tier (Servlets and JSPs), a cluster for Stateless EJBs, a cluster for Entity Beans, and a cluster for the database. And as you can imagine, load balancing, failover and sticky sessions for every tier were loaded with application servers. This e-commerce website went live... and it worked!

Then came Struts, Spring and Hibernate. Full J2EE application servers shrank down to servlet containers such as Tomcat or Jetty. We could see things moving, such as architectures becoming stateless, failover being abandoned, migrations from SOAP to REST and mobile devices taking over web crawling. Then came the *Internet of Things* (IoT), the cloud, microservices, *Function as a Service* (FaaS), and it never stops moving. Other things didn't change, like the good old *Gang of Four* design patterns, architecture design patterns, unit testing frameworks and building tools. We reinvented some wheels and gave them different names, but we also learnt dozens of new promising programming languages (running on top of the JVM or not) and agile techniques. Thanks to these evolutions that I have witnessed, today you can sit down, read this fascicle and write some code.

Where Does This Fascicle Come From?

Involved in J2EE since 1998, I followed its evolution and joined the Java EE expert group from version 6 to version 8. During that time, I wrote a book in French called "*Java EE 5*".[14] The book was published by a French editor and got noticed. I was then contacted by Apress, an American editor, to work on an English version. I liked the challenge. So, I changed the structure of the book, updated it, translated it, and I ended up with a "*Beginning Java EE 6*" book. A few years later, Java EE 7 was released, so I updated my book, added a few extra chapters, and ended up with a "*Beginning Java EE 7*" that was 500 pages long.[15]. This process of writing got a bit painful (some text editors shouldn't be used to write books), inflexible (it's hard to update a paper book frequently) and I also had some arguments with my editor.[16]

Parallel to that, the history of Java EE 8 was also somewhat painful and long.[17] I was still part of the Expert Group, but nobody really knew why the experts' mailing list was so quiet. No real exchange, no real vision, no real challenges. That's when I decided not to work on a Java EE 8 book. But the community said otherwise. I started receiving emails about updating my book. I used to always meet someone at a conference going "*Hey, Antonio, when is your next book coming out?*" My answer was "*No way!*"

I decided to take stock. What was holding me back from writing? Clearly it was my editor and Java EE 8. So, I decided to get rid of both. I extracted the chapters I wanted from my Java EE 7 book and updated them. That's where the idea of writing "*fascicles*", instead of an entire book, came from. Then, I looked at self-publishing, and here I am at Amazon Kindle Publishing.[18]

Bean Validation took up a single chapter of my "Beginning Java EE 7" and was 34 pages long. It was about Bean Validation 1.1. Since then, this specification has evolved towards a version 2.0 and is used in many different frameworks. I even created an entire online course for PluralSight.[19] And today, I still use Bean Validation extensively in my projects.

I hope you'll find this fascicle useful.

Who Is This Fascicle For?

Bean Validation has its genesis in the Hibernate community with Hibernate Validator. It was then specified in the JCP and became part of the Java EE platform. But Hibernate Validator always evolved outside the JCP while making it easy for other technologies to integrate.

So, this fascicle is for the Java community as a whole. If you come from Java EE, you will be, of course, very familiar with Bean Validation. But this fascicle is also meant to be used by the Spring community. Spring has embraced Bean Validation since the beginning. So, all of the explanations and examples you'll see in this fascicle work out of the box with Spring, Java EE and other Java technologies.

And of course, Bean Validation works on plain vanilla Java SE, so any Java developer can benefit from it. The only requirement to follow and fully understand this fascicle is to know Java.

How Is This Fascicle Structured?

This fascicle concentrates on Bean Validation 2.0. Its structure will help you to discover this technology as well as helping you to further dive into it if you already have some experience of it.

This fascicle starts with Chapter 1, *First Step with Bean Validation* by showing a few lines of Bean Validation code.

Chapter 2, *Understanding Bean Validation* briefly presents Bean Validation, the problems it addresses and explains the common concerns discussed throughout the fascicle. This chapter also looks at the standardisation side of this technology and where it comes from.

Chapter 3, *Getting Started* is all about showing some basic code of Bean Validation and introducing its main APIs and deployment descriptors.

Chapter 4, *Applying Constraints* explains how you apply built-in constraints to attributes, containers and methods, and how to handle error messages.

Once you constrain your model, you need to validate it. Chapter 5, *Validating Constraints* covers validation and how you make sure the data passed to attributes or methods is valid. The chapter also covers cascade validation.

Built-in constraints are not always enough. Comes a time where you need to create your own constraints. Chapter 6, *Writing Constraints* looks into how a constraint is defined.

Chapter 7, *Advanced Topics* covers some advanced topics such as constraint inheritance or grouping constraints together.

Chapter 8, *Integrating Bean Validation with Other Technologies* shows how to integrate Bean Validation with other technologies such as JPA, JSF, CDI, JAX-RS and Spring.

In Chapter 9, *Putting It All Together*, you'll build a more complex application with most of the concepts that have been introduced throughout this fascicle.

Chapter 10, *Summary* wraps up with a summary of what you've learnt in this fascicle.

Appendix A, *Setting up the Development Environment on macOS* highlights the tools used throughout the fascicle and how to install them.

Bean Validation 2.0 has a long history of specifications behind it. Appendix B, *Bean Validation Specification Versions* lists all the revisions of this specification.

Appendix C points to some external references which are worth reading if you want to know more about Bean Validation.

Thanks to self-publication and electronic format, I can update this fascicle regularly when typos or bugs are discovered. Appendix D, *Revisions of the Fascicle* gives you the revision notes of each version of this fascicle.

This is not the only fascicle I have written. You'll find a description of the other fascicles I wrote and online courses I created in Appendix E:

- *Understanding Bean Validation 2.0*
- *Understanding JPA 2.2*
- *Understanding Quarkus 2.x*
- *Practising Quarkus 2.x*

Conventions

This fascicle uses a diverse range of languages, mostly Java, but also JSON, XML, YAML or shell scripts. Each code example is displayed appropriately and appears in `fixed-width font`. All the included code comes from a public Git repository and is continuously tested. Therefore, you shouldn't have any problem with code that is not syntactically correct. In some cases, the original source code has been specially formatted to fit within the available page space, with additional line breaks or modified indentation. To increase readability, some examples omit code where it is seen as unnecessary. But always remember that you can find the entire code online at https://github.com/agoncal/agoncal-fascicle-bean-validation/tree/2.0.

Italics are used to *highlight an important word for the first time*, or to give the definition of an abbreviation or *acronym*. Bold is **rarely used**.

 Some useful information.

 Something you really should do if you want the code to work properly.

 Warns you of a possible technical problem.

The Sample Application

Throughout the book, you will see snippets of code all belonging to the Vintage Store application. I created this application for my very first book, and I still use it as an example. This application is an e-commerce website allowing users to browse a catalogue of vintage stuff (vinyl, tapes, books and CDs). Using a shopping cart, they can add or remove items as they browse the catalogue and then check out so that they can pay and obtain a purchase order. The application has external interactions with a bank system to validate credit card numbers.

The actors interacting with the system are:

- *Employees* of the company who need to manage both the catalogue of items and the customers' details. They can also browse the purchase orders.

- *Users* who are anonymous persons visiting the website and who are consulting the catalogue of books and CDs. If they want to buy an item, they need to create an account to become customers.

- *Customers* who can login to the system, browse the catalogue, update their account details, and buy items online.

- The external *Bank* to which the system delegates credit card validations.

Figure 1 depicts the use case diagram which describes the system's actors and functionalities.

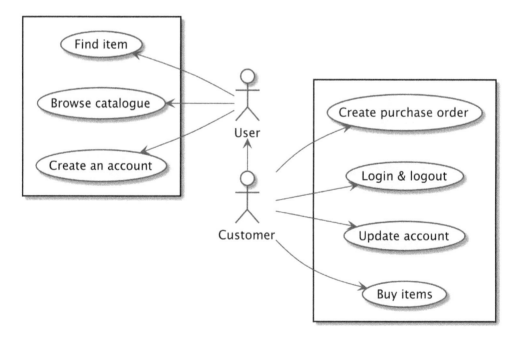

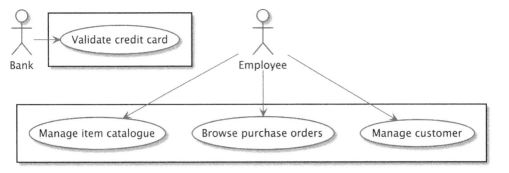

Figure 1. Use case diagram of the Vintage Store application

The Vintage Store application manipulates a few domain objects that are described in Figure 2. Vinyl, tapes, books and CDs, of course, but also chapters, authors, purchase orders, invoices and shopping carts. Don't spend too much time on this diagram for now as you will come across most of these objects throughout this fascicle.

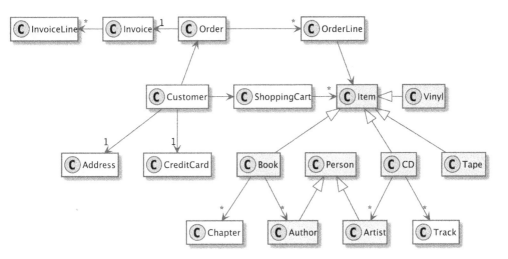

Figure 2. Class diagram of the Vintage Store application

 The code you'll see in this fascicle gets its inspiration from the Vintage Store application, but it's not the original application per-se. You can download the code of the original application if you want, but it's not necessary in order to follow the code of this fascicle.[20]

Downloading and Running the Code

The source code of the examples in the fascicle is available from a public Git repository and can be cloned, downloaded or browsed online at https://github.com/agoncal/agoncal-fascicle-bean-validation/tree/2.0. The code has been developed and tested on the macOS platform but should also work on Windows or Linux. The examples used in this fascicle are designed to be compiled with Java 11, to be built with Maven 3.6.x and to be tested with JUnit 5.x and to store data in an H2 database. Appendix A shows you how to install all of these software packages which will be used in most of the chapters to build, run and test the code.

Getting Help

Having trouble with the code, the content or the structure of the fascicle? Didn't understand something? Not clear enough? I am here to help! Do not hesitate to report issues or any questions at https://github.com/agoncal/agoncal-fascicle-bean-validation/issues. I'll do my best to answer them. This will also allow me to improve the content of this fascicle, and upload a new version through Amazon Kindle Publishing.

Contacting the Author

If you have any questions about the content of this fascicle, please use the instructions above and use the GitHub issue tracker. But if you feel like contacting me, drop me an email at agoncal.fascicle@gmail.com **or a tweet at** @agoncal. You can also visit my blog at:

- www.antoniogoncalves.org

- agoncal.teachable.com

[14] Autonio's books http://amazon.com/author/agoncal

[15] My Java EE Books https://antoniogoncalves.org/category/books

[16] The Uncensored Java EE 7 Book https://antoniogoncalves.org/2014/09/16/the-uncensored-java-ee-7-book

[17] Opening Up Java EE https://blogs.oracle.com/theaquarium/opening-up-ee-update

[18] Amazon Kindle Publishing https://kdp.amazon.com

[19] Bean Validation course on PluralSight https://app.pluralsight.com/library/courses/bean-validation

[20] Code of the Vintage Store application https://github.com/agoncal/agoncal-application-cdbookstore

Chapter 1. First Step with Bean Validation

If you are reading this fascicle, it's because you are a developer. And like most developers, when you learn a new technology or framework, you like to see some code first. So here is the very first step with Bean Validation.

Listing 1 shows a Java class representing the author of a book. An author has a first name, a last name, a biography and an email address.

Listing 1. Java Class with Bean Validation Annotations

```java
public class Author {

    @NotNull @Size(min = 2, max = 50)
    private String firstName;
    @NotNull
    private String lastName;
    @Size(max = 2000)
    private String bio;
    @Email
    private String email;

    // Constructors, getters, setters
}
```

If you look more carefully at Listing 1, you can see a few annotations: @NotNull, @Size and @Email. What do you think they do? Let me give you a hint. In Listing 2 we give the author a first name and a last name, and when we validate the author object, we get an empty set of constraint violations. This means that there is no constraint violated, therefore, the author object is valid.

Listing 2. The Author is Valid

```java
Author author = new Author().firstName("Adams").lastName("Douglas");

Set<ConstraintViolation<Author>> violations = validator.validate(author);
assertTrue(violations.isEmpty());
```

Look at what happens in Listing 3. This time, we give the author a wrong email address, and when we validate it, the size of the set of constraint violations is equal to one. And if we dive into the APIs, we can see that there is an error message "must be a well-formed email address" with the wrong value "wrong".

Listing 3. The Email of the Author Is Invalid

```
Author author = new Author().firstName("Adams").lastName("Douglas").email("wrong");

Set<ConstraintViolation<Author>> violations = validator.validate(author);
assertEquals(1, violations.size());

ConstraintViolation<Author> violation = violations.iterator().next();
assertEquals("must be a well-formed email address", violation.getMessage());
assertEquals("wrong", violation.getInvalidValue());
assertEquals("email", violation.getPropertyPath().toString());
```

You didn't understand all the code? You did understand it but you feel there is more to it than that? The fascicle you have in your hands is all about Bean Validation. Thanks to the chapters that follow, you will understand the basics of this technology and will have plenty of examples so that you can dive into more complex topics.

Chapter 2. Understanding Bean Validation

In the previous *First Step with Bean Validation* chapter, you've already seen some code. But before going further into more code, we need to step back and define some concepts. This *Understanding* chapter gives you some terminology that will be used in the rest of the fascicle so you don't get lost.

Validating data is a common concern that is spread across several, if not all, layers of today's applications (from presentation to persistence). Because processing, storing, and retrieving valid data is crucial for an application, each layer defines validation rules in its own way. Often the same validation logic is implemented in each layer, proving to be time-consuming, harder to maintain, and error prone. To avoid duplication of these validations in each layer, developers often bundle validation logic directly into the domain model, cluttering domain classes with validation code that is, in fact, metadata about the class itself.

Bean Validation solves the problem of code duplication by allowing developers to write a constraint once, use it, and validate it in any layer. Bean Validation implements a constraint in plain Java code and then defines it by an annotation (metadata). This annotation can then be used on your bean, properties, constructors, method parameters, and return value. In a very elegant yet powerful way, Bean Validation exposes a simple API to help developers write and reuse business logic constraints.

2.1. Understanding Constraints and Validation

Application developers spend a considerable amount of time making sure the data they process and store is valid. They write data constraints, apply these constraints to their logic and model, and make sure the different layers validate these constraints in a consistent manner. This means applying these constraints in their client application (e.g. web browser, JavaFX etc.), presentation layer, business logic layer, domain model (a.k.a. business model), database schema, and, to some degree, the interoperability layer (see Figure 3). And, of course, for consistency, they have to keep all these rules synchronised across all layers.

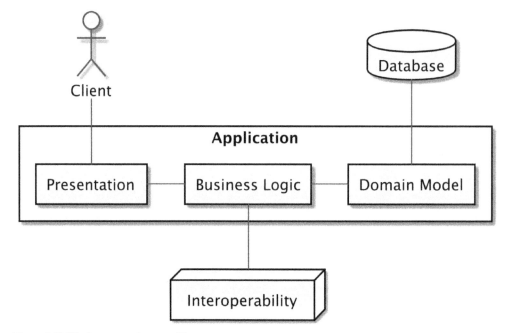

Figure 3. Validation occurs in several layers

In heterogeneous applications, developers have to deal with several technologies and languages. So even a simple validation rule, such as *"this piece of data is mandatory and cannot be null,"* has to be expressed differently in Java, JavaScript, database schema, or XML schema.

2.1.1. Application

No matter if you develop a one tier or a multi-tier application, you need to make sure the data you process is correct. For example, if the delivery address of the purchase order is empty, you would never be able to ship the items to your customer. In Java you will commonly write code that checks if an entry is valid (`if (order.getDeliveryAddress() == null)`) and throws an exception or asks for feedback to correct it. Application-level validation is able to provide finer-grained control and allows more complex constraints like "Is this date a public holiday in Portugal?" or "Is the customer's annual total bill amount greater than the average?"

Application-level validation may reside in multiple places to ensure that the data is correct:

- *Presentation layer*: In this layer you validate the data because the data could have been sent from several clients (a web browser, a mobile application, or a desktop application) and you want to give your users some quick feedback.

- *Business logic layer*: This layer orchestrates the calls to your internal and external services, and to your domain model so the processed data has to be valid.

- *Domain model layer*: This layer usually maps your business model to the database, so you need to validate it before storing the data.

In a complex application, you will repeat the exact same constraint in several layers, resulting in a large amount of code duplication.

2.1.2. Database

At the end of the day, what you really want is to store valid data in your database so the data can be processed later. Some constraints can be enforced by relational databases as they use schemas. A *Data Definition Language* (DDL, or data description language) uses a syntax for defining and constraining database structures. You can then make sure data in a column cannot be null (NOT NULL), has to be numerical (INTEGER), or must have a maximum length (VARCHAR(20)). In this last example, trying to insert a 30-character-long string into a column will fail.

However, letting the database handle validation has several drawbacks. It has a performance cost and error messages are out of context. Invalid data must cross all application layers before reaching the remote database server, which will then handle the validation before sending back an error. At the database level, constraints are only aware of the data, not what the user is doing. So, error messages are not aware of the context and cannot be very explicit. That's why we tend to validate the data earlier in the application or in the client.

2.1.3. Client

On the client side, it is important to validate data so the users are quickly informed that they have entered wrong data. It reduces the number of roundtrips to the server and provides a better user experience through early error feedback. It is crucial when developing mobile applications that may use a low-bandwidth network connection.

In a typical web application, for example, JavaScript is executed in the browser for simple field-level validations and the server-side layer is used for more complex business rule validations. Also remember that client side validation can be easily bypassed just by disabling JavaScript, so it's not something to rely on (that's why it's good to also keep the server-side validation). Native applications written in Java (Swing, Android mobile applications, JavaFX) can use the full power of the Java language to write and validate data.

2.1.4. Interoperability

Often applications need to exchange data with external partners and external systems. These business-to-business applications receive data in any kind of format, process it, store it, and send it back to their partner. Validating custom formats can be a complex and expensive task. Nowadays, we exchange data between heterogeneous systems in XML, JSON or YAML.

Like databases that use DDL to define their structure, XML can use XSD (XML Schema Definition) to constrain XML documents.[21] XSD expresses a set of rules to which an XML document must conform in order to be considered valid according to that schema. XML parsing and validation is a common task and easy to do with Java frameworks.

JSON also has schema definition language called JSON Schema.[22] It's newer than XML but the purpose is the same: validating data that is exchanged between peers.

2.2. Bean Validation Overview

Validating data is a common task that developers have to do and it is spread throughout all layers of an application (from client to database). This common practice is time-consuming, error prone, and hard to maintain in the long run. Besides, some of these constraints are so frequently used that they could be considered standard (checking for a null value, size, range, etc.). It would be good to be able to centralise these constraints in one place and share them across layers. That's where Bean Validation comes into play.

Bean Validation allows you to write a constraint once and reuse it in different application layers.[23] It is layer agnostic, meaning that the same constraint can be used from the presentation to the business model layer. Bean Validation is available for server-side applications as well as rich Java client graphical interfaces (Swing, Android, JavaFX etc.).

Bean Validation allows you to apply already-defined common constraints to your application, and also to write your own validation rules in order to validate beans, attributes, constructors, method return values and parameters. The API is very easy to use and flexible as it encourages you to define your constraints using annotations or XML descriptors.

Bean Validation is just a specification that is part of Java EE and is governed by the JCP (*Java Community Process*). It is then implemented by frameworks such as Hibernate Validator, Apache BVal or Sourceforge OVal.

2.2.1. A Brief History of Bean Validation

Developers have been constraining and validating their business models since Java was first developed. Homemade code and frameworks gave birth to practices that were implemented in early open source projects. For example, back in 2000, Struts, the famous Web MVC framework, already implemented a user input validation.[24] But we had to wait some time for validation frameworks dedicated solely to Java (and not just web interaction) to appear. The best known are probably Commons Validator from the Apache Commons, and Hibernate Validator.[25] Others are iScreen, OVal, and the ubiquitous Spring framework that came with its own validation package (and then integrated with Bean Validation).

Inspired by these validation frameworks, Bean Validation 1.0 (JSR 303) was first standardised by the JCP in 2009 and got included in Java EE 6.[26] Later versions followed the same path: Bean Validation 1.1 was added to Java EE 7 and Bean Validation 2.0 to Java EE 8.

2.2.2. JCP and Eclipse Foundation

The JCP (*Java Community Process*) is an open organisation, created in 1998 by Sun Microsystems, that is involved in the definition of future versions and features of the Java platform.[27] When the need for standardising an existing component or API is identified, the initiator (a.k.a. specification lead) creates a JSR (*Java Specification Request*) and forms a group of experts. This group, made up of company representatives, organisations, universities, and private individuals, is responsible for the development of the JSR and has to deliver:

- One or more specifications that explain the details and define the fundamentals of the JSR,
- A *Reference Implementation* (RI), which is an actual implementation of the specification, and
- A *Technology Compatibility Kit* (TCK), which is a set of tests every implementation needs to pass before claiming to conform to the specification.

Once approved by the *Executive Committee* (EC), the specification is released to the community for other projects to implement.

This is exactly the standardisation process that followed Bean Validation 2.0. It has been standardised under JSR 380, has a reference implementation (Hibernate Validator) and has a TCK.[28]

In 2017, most Java EE specifications were moved from the JCP to the Eclipse Foundation (including the Bean Validation specification).[29]

The *Eclipse Foundation* is an independent, non-profit entity that acts as a steward for the Eclipse open source software development community.[30] The Foundation focuses on key services such as: intellectual property management, ecosystem development, development process, and IT infrastructure. It was created by IBM in 2001 and is now supported by a consortium of several software vendors (Red Hat, Huawei, Bosch, Fujitsu, SAP, Oracle, etc.).

2.2.3. Java EE and Jakarta EE

Even if Bean Validation does not rely on Java EE, it is strongly correlated with this platform. So, it is worth mentioning Java EE in a Bean Validation fascicle.

Created in 1998, Java EE (*Java Enterprise Edition*) can be seen as an extension of the *Java Standard Edition* (Java SE).[31] It is a set of specifications intended for enterprise applications in order to facilitate the development of distributed, transactional, and secure applications. It is developed using the *Java Community Process*, with contributions from industry experts and commercial and open source organisations.[32]

In 2017, with version 8 of the platform, Java EE was donated to the Eclipse Foundation and renamed *Jakarta EE*.[33] Jakarta EE is the name of the platform governed by the Jakarta EE Working Group.[34] The first version is Jakarta EE 8, which is based on the Java EE 8 technologies. Future versions will not be driven by the JCP but through the open *Eclipse Foundation*.

2.2.4. Expression Language

Bean Validation relies on the Expression Language specification. It is used to interpolate error messages when a constraint is violated, as you will see in a later chapter.

EL, or *Expression Language*, is a specification defined by the JCP (JSR 341).[35] Originally inspired by both ECMAScript and XPath, the Expression Language was created to make it easy for developers to access and manipulate data in web applications without having to master the complexity associated with programming languages such as Java and JavaScript. Its syntax is quite simple and is restricted to the evaluation of expressions, variables and nested properties. It then became richer and you can now use its logical, arithmetic, conditional, and empty operators.

2.2.5. What's New in Bean Validation 2.0?

Bean Validation 2.0 is described under the JSR 380 and was released in 2017.[36] This major release brings many new features and improves existing ones.[37] The major new features are:

- Adds support for Java SE 8 (the requirement of Java 8 was the motivation behind creating a major version 2.0 instead of a 1.2).

- Validation annotations can be added to containers such as collections (e.g. `List<@Positive Integer> positiveNumbers`) and `java.util.Optional`.

- New built-in constraints: `@Email`, `@NotEmpty`, `@NotBlank`, `@Positive`, `@PositiveOrZero`, `@Negative`, `@NegativeOrZero`, `@PastOrPresent` and `@FutureOrPresent`.

- All built-in constraints are marked as `@Repeatable`.

- Support for `java.util.Optional`.

- Support for the new date/time data types (JSR 310).[38]

Most of these novelties will be discussed in the chapters that follow.

 Appendix B lists all the revisions and major changes of the Bean Validation specification.

2.2.6. Implementations

Hibernate Validator is the open source reference implementation of Bean Validation.[39] The project was originally launched in Hibernate Annotations in 2005 by JBoss, became an independent project in 2007, and became the reference implementation for Bean Validation 1.0 (JSR 303) in 2009 (with Hibernate Validator 4). Today, Hibernate Validator 6.x implements Bean Validation 2.0. It also adds specific features, which include a fail fast mode (return from the current validation as soon as the first constraint violation occurs), a programmatic constraint configuration API, and extra built-in constraints.

 The code in this fascicle uses the standard Bean Validation APIs. As for the implementation, it uses Hibernate Validator.

At the time of writing this fascicle, Hibernate Validator is the only Bean Validation 2.0 compliant implementation. Apache BVal implements Bean Validation 1.1 and will probably be in line to get the 2.0 certification.[40] Sourceforge OVal doesn't implement the full Bean Validation specification but comes with a configurer that can translate the standard Bean Validation constraints into equivalent OVal constraints.[41]

As you can see, despite the reference implementation (Hibernate Validator), you have several implementations to choose from.

[21] XSD https://www.w3.org/TR/xmlschema11-1

[22] JSON Schema http://json-schema.org

[23] Bean Validation https://jcp.org/en/jsr/detail?id=380

[24] Struts https://struts.apache.org

[25] Apache Commons Validator https://commons.apache.org/proper/commons-validator

[26] JSR 303 https://jcp.org/en/jsr/detail?id=303

[27] JCP https://jcp.org

[28] Bean Validation https://jcp.org/en/jsr/detail?id=380

[29] Eclipse Foundation https://www.eclipse.org/org/foundation

[30] Eclipse Foundation https://www.eclipse.org/org/foundation

[31] Jakarta EE https://en.wikipedia.org/wiki/Jakarta_EE

[32] JCP https://jcp.org

[33] Eclipse Foundation https://www.eclipse.org/org/foundation/

[34] Jakarta EE https://jakarta.ee

[35] Expression Language https://jcp.org/en/jsr/detail?id=341

[36] JSR 380 https://jcp.org/en/jsr/detail?id=380

[37] Changes between Bean Validation 2.0 and 1.1 http://beanvalidation.org/2.0/#changes-between-bean-validation-2-0-and-1-1

[38] JSR 310 https://jcp.org/en/jsr/detail?id=310

[39] Hibernate Validator http://hibernate.org/validator

[40] BVal http://bval.apache.org

[41] OVal http://oval.sourceforge.net

Chapter 3. Getting Started

In the previous chapter, you learnt about validation and why it is important to process valid data. You've also looked at what Bean Validation is and where it comes from. Time to see some code.

To get started with a new technology, there is nothing better than a simple "*Hello World*" kind of example. In this *Getting Started* chapter, you will be developing your very first Bean Validation sample application. It is a simple application made up of only a few classes with not much technical complexity. The idea is to develop something simple to understand and to set up so that you are sure you have the basis to follow the chapters coming up.

 Make sure your development environment is set up to execute the code in this chapter. You can go to Appendix A to check that you have all the required tools installed, in particular JDK 11.0.10 or higher and Maven 3.6.x or higher. The code in this chapter can be found at https://github.com/agoncal/agoncal-fascicle-bean-validation/tree/2.0/getting-started

3.1. Developing Your First Bean Validation Application

Let's develop a simple application that highlights some of the key features of Bean Validation. In this chapter, we'll use a Maven directory structure with an `Artist` class and an `ArtistTest` test class:

- `pom.xml`: At the root of the project, we find the Maven `pom.xml` file defining all the dependencies.
- `Artist.java`: The artist class with a set of attributes annotated with Bean Validation constraint annotations.
- `ArtistTest.java`: Test class with a set of test cases validating valid and invalid data.

The Maven directory structure ensures we put the business code under `src/main/java` while the test code goes under `src/test/java`.

```
.
├── src
│   ├── main
│   │   └── java
│   │       └── org/agoncal/fascicle/beanvalidation/gettingstarted
│   │           └── Artist.java
│   └── test
│       └── java
│           └── org/agoncal/fascicle/beanvalidation/gettingstarted
│               └── ArtistTest.java
└── pom.xml
```

We use Maven to build this project because it is the most commonly used build system these days.[42] Plus, we can use Maven in the command line and most IDEs support it.

3.1.1. Setting up the Maven Dependencies

We need to start by creating a pom.xml file. The pom.xml is the fundamental unit of work in Maven that will be used to build our project. Listing 4 shows the header of the pom.xml with just the groupId and artifactId.

Listing 4. Header of the pom.xml

```xml
<project xmlns:xsi="http://www.w3.org/2001/XMLSchema-instance"
         xmlns="http://maven.apache.org/POM/4.0.0"
         xsi:schemaLocation="http://maven.apache.org/POM/4.0.0
 http://maven.apache.org/xsd/maven-4.0.0.xsd">
   <modelVersion>4.0.0</modelVersion>

   <groupId>org.agoncal.fascicle.bean-validation</groupId>
   <artifactId>getting-started</artifactId>
   <version>2.0</version>

   <properties>
      <maven.compiler.source>11</maven.compiler.source>
      <maven.compiler.target>11</maven.compiler.target>
      <project.build.sourceEncoding>UTF-8</project.build.sourceEncoding>
      <project.reporting.outputEncoding>UTF-8</project.reporting.outputEncoding>
   </properties>
```

Listing 5 gives us all the required dependencies to compile and execute the code. Basically, the only Bean Validation dependencies we need here are the ones from Hibernate Validator (by pulling the reference implementation org.hibernate.validator:hibernate-validator) as well as an Expression Language (JSR 341) implementation (org.glassfish:javax.el) used by Hibernate Validator to generate violation messages when a constraint fails.

Listing 5. Bean Validation Dependencies

```xml
<dependencies>
  <dependency>
    <groupId>org.hibernate.validator</groupId>
    <artifactId>hibernate-validator</artifactId>
    <version>6.2.0.Final</version>
  </dependency>
  <dependency>
    <groupId>org.glassfish</groupId>
    <artifactId>javax.el</artifactId>
    <version>3.0.1-b12</version>
  </dependency>
</dependencies>
```

We use JUnit 5.x to run our tests.[13] As shown in Listing 6, we need to include the org.junit.jupiter dependency whose scope is set to test and to setup the maven-surefire-plugin so a simple mvn test command will execute the tests.

Listing 6. Test Dependencies

```xml
    <dependency>
      <groupId>org.junit.jupiter</groupId>
      <artifactId>junit-jupiter-engine</artifactId>
      <version>5.7.1</version>
      <scope>test</scope>
    </dependency>
  </dependencies>

  <build>
    <plugins>
      <plugin>
        <groupId>org.apache.maven.plugins</groupId>
        <artifactId>maven-surefire-plugin</artifactId>
        <version>3.0.0-M5</version>
      </plugin>
    </plugins>
  </build>
</project>
```

 At this point, you can import the Maven project into an IDE (most modern Java IDEs include built-in support for Maven).

If you run `mvn dependency:tree`, you will see in Listing 7 that several dependencies were not explicitly defined in the `pom.xml` in Listing 5. That's because Maven transitively pulls all the needed dependencies automatically. That's why we end up with the Bean Validation API (`javax.validation:validation-api`) for example.

Listing 7. Maven Dependencies Tree

```
+- org.hibernate.validator:hibernate-validator:jar:6.0.5.Final:compile
|  +- javax.validation:validation-api:jar:2.0.0.Final:compile
|  +- org.jboss.logging:jboss-logging:jar:3.3.0.Final:compile
|  \- com.fasterxml:classmate:jar:1.3.1:compile
+- org.glassfish:javax.el:jar:3.0.1-b08:compile
\- org.junit.jupiter:junit-jupiter-engine:jar:5.0.2:test
   +- org.junit.platform:junit-platform-engine:jar:1.0.2:test
   |  +- org.junit.platform:junit-platform-commons:jar:1.0.2:test
   |  \- org.opentest4j:opentest4j:jar:1.0.0:test
   \- org.junit.jupiter:junit-jupiter-api:jar:5.0.2:test
```

 Appendix A has an entire chapter on Maven, explaining the scopes (runtime, test etc.) and the goals you can use on a `pom.xml`. Please refer to it if you need more in-depth information on Maven.

3.1.2. Applying Constraints

Let's dive into an example to see how to apply constraints. In Listing 8, we have an Artist class with several attributes. An artist who appears on a CD album has a first name, a last name, an email address, a biography and a date of birth. This code is very straightforward. The Artist class does not extend any class nor does it implement any interface. It has a default constructor, getters and setters. The only difference with plain Java code and this class, is the usage of annotations on these attributes.

Listing 8. The Artist Class Annotated with Constraints

```java
public class Artist {

    @NotNull
    private String firstName;

    @NotNull
    private String lastName;

    @Email
    private String email;

    @Size(max = 2000)
    private String bio;

    @Past
    private LocalDate dateOfBirth;

    // Constructors, getters, setters
}
```

The @NotNull, @Email, @Size and @Past annotations are used to declare the constraints which should be applied to the attributes of an Artist instance:

- The artist first name and last name must not be null,
- The email property should be a valid email address,
- The biography can be null, but if it's not, its size must be lower than 2000 characters long, and
- The date of birth must be in the past.

This code is very straightforward to read. The Bean Validation annotations bring semantic to these attributes ("the email attribute is not just a String, it is a String that must have a valid @Email address") as well as a runtime API to validate the values of these attributes.

3.1.3. Validating Constraints

We use the javax.validation.Validator API to validate these constraints. To demonstrate this, let's have a look at a simple unit test: ArtistTest.

Listing 9. Test Class Initialising the Bean Validation Container

```java
public class ArtistTest {

  private static ValidatorFactory vf;
  private static Validator validator;

  @BeforeAll
  static void init() {
    vf = Validation.buildDefaultValidatorFactory();
    validator = vf.getValidator();
  }

  @AfterAll
  static void close() {
    if (vf != null) vf.close();
  }
```

In Listing 9 we define two attributes (ValidatorFactory vf and Validator validator) that are initialised once (thanks to the JUnit @BeforeAll annotation) in the init() method. In the init() method, a Validator instance is retrieved from the ValidatorFactory. Validator instances are thread-safe and may be reused multiple times. The ValidatorFactory is closed at the end of the test case (@AfterAll) in the close() method.

Now, let's use the Validator API to validate an artist.

Listing 10. Test Case with Valid Data

```java
@Test
void shouldRaiseNoConstraintViolation() {

  Artist artist = new Artist().firstName("Adams").lastName("Douglas");

  Set<ConstraintViolation<Artist>> violations = validator.validate(artist);
  assertTrue(violations.isEmpty());
}
```

In Listing 10, we create an instance of a valid artist with a valid first name and last name. The validate() method returns a set of ConstraintViolation instances, each representing a constraint that has been violated. In this case, the set is empty: no constraint has been violated, the artist object contains valid data.

Listing 11. One Constraint Violation Due to Null Firstname

```java
@Test
void shouldRaiseConstraintViolationCauseFirstNameIsNull() {

    Artist artist = new Artist().firstName(null).lastName("Douglas");

    Set<ConstraintViolation<Artist>> violations = validator.validate(artist);
    assertEquals(1, violations.size());
}
```

In Listing 11, we create an `artist` object with a `null` first name. The `@NotNull` constraint on `firstName` attribute is violated, therefore, the size of the `violations` set is one.

Listing 12. One Constraint Violation Due to Invalid Email

```java
@Test
void shouldRaiseConstraintViolationCauseInvalidEmail() {

    Artist artist = new Artist().firstName("Adams").lastName("Douglas").email("wrong");

    Set<ConstraintViolation<Artist>> violations = validator.validate(artist);
    assertEquals(1, violations.size());

    ConstraintViolation<Artist> violation = violations.iterator().next();
    assertEquals("must be a well-formed email address", violation.getMessage());
    assertEquals("wrong", violation.getInvalidValue());
    assertEquals("email", violation.getPropertyPath().toString());
}
```

In Listing 12, we create a test case to validate that an email address has to be well formed. Here, the `email` attribute is set to `wrong`, therefore, the size of the `violations` set is one. Notice that we iterate through this set so we can get more information about the violation. Here, we check that the error message is "must be a well-formed email address" and that the value is "wrong". We can also get specific information about the object itself or the attribute (`violation.getPropertyPath()` returns the property with invalid value: `email`).

Listing 13. Two Constraint Violations Due to Invalid Email and Invalid Date

```java
@Test
void shouldRaiseTwoConstraintViolationsCauseInvalidEmailAndFutureDate() {

    LocalDate dateOfBirth = LocalDate.of(2678, 12, 01);
    Artist artist = new Artist().firstName("Adams").lastName("Douglas").email("wrong")
.dateOfBirth(dateOfBirth);

    Set<ConstraintViolation<Artist>> violations = validator.validate(artist);
    assertEquals(2, violations.size());
}
```

In Listing 13, we first set a birth date in the future (1st of December 2678) and a wrong email address. Once the Artist class is validated, Bean Validation reports that we violate two constraints: the @Email constraint and the @Past constraint on dateOfBirth. @Past makes sure that the date is earlier than today, which makes sense for a date of birth.

In this test, besides some JUnit APIs, we use classes from the javax.validation package which are provided by the Bean Validation API and not the reference implementation of Hibernate Validator (refer to Listing 7); meaning that this code should work with the other Bean Validation implementations we saw earlier in the previous chapter.

3.1.4. Running the Tests

We have the Artist class, its test case (ArtistTest) and the pom.xml. Now it is the time to run the tests. Depending on the IDE you use, executing the tests can be as simple as clicking on a button.

But thanks to Maven, we can execute them on a command line using the mvn test command. It is enough to compile the classes and run the tests so you should see the following output:

```
[INFO] -----------------------
[INFO] Building Getting Started
[INFO] -----------------------
[INFO]
[INFO] --- maven-compiler-plugin:3.7.0:compile (default-compile)
[INFO]
[INFO] --- maven-surefire-plugin:2.20:test (default-test)
[INFO]
[INFO] -----------
[INFO]  T E S T S
[INFO] -----------
[INFO] Running org.agoncal.fascicle.beanvalidation.gettingstarted.ArtistTest
[INFO] Tests run: 4, Failures: 0, Errors: 0, Skipped: 0, Time elapsed: 0.365 s
[INFO]
[INFO] Results:
[INFO]
[INFO] Tests run: 4, Failures: 0, Errors: 0, Skipped: 0
[INFO]
[INFO] -------------
[INFO] BUILD SUCCESS
[INFO] -------------
```

What's really important is the result: 4 tests were run and all of them passed. If you have the same output, it means your environment is up and running and that you are ready for more Bean Validation code.

3.2. A Closer Look at Bean Validation

Now that you've run your first test, let's have a closer look at Bean Validation. This will give you some terminology that will be used in the chapters that follow.

3.2.1. Bean Validation Packages

The Bean Validation APIs and annotations are all defined under the `javax.validation` package. Table 1 lists the main subpackages defined in Bean Validation 2.0 (under the root `javax.validation` package).[14]

Table 1. Main javax.validation Subpackages

Subpackage	Description
root	Root package of the Bean Validation APIs
bootstrap	Classes used to bootstrap Bean Validation and to create a provider agnostic configuration
constraints	This package contains all the built-in constraints
constraintvalidation	Package containing constructs specific to constraint validators
executable	Package related to the control and execution of validation on constructors and methods
groups	Bean Validation groups for defining a subset of constraints
metadata	Metadata repository for all defined constraints and query API
spi	Internal SPIs (*Service Provider Interfaces*) implemented by the provider
valueextraction	Package dedicated to extracting values to validate container elements

3.2.2. Main Bean Validation APIs

The class diagram in Figure 4 highlights the main Bean Validation APIs.

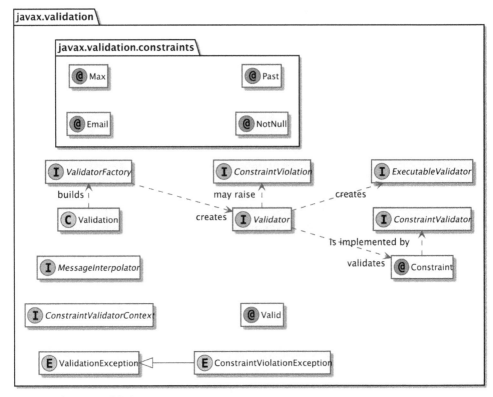

Figure 4. Main Bean Validation APIs

Of course there are many more APIs in Bean Validation as you will see in the chapters that follow. But Table 2 lists the main ones.

Table 2. Main Bean Validation APIs

API	Description
Validation	This class is the entry point for Bean Validation and is used to build a ValidatorFactory
ValidatorFactory	This interface acts as a factory for returning initialised Validator instances
Validator	The implementation of this interface is used to validate bean instances
ExecutableValidator	Validates parameters and return values of methods and constructors
ConstraintViolation	Describes a constraint violation exposing the constraint violation context as well as the message describing the violation
ConstraintValidator	Defines the logic to validate a given @Constraint
MessageInterpolator	Builds a given constraint violation message when a constraint fails
ConstraintValidatorContext	Provides contextual data and operation when executing a given constraint validator
ValidationException	Base exception of all Bean Validation "expected" problems

API	Description
`ConstraintViolationExc eption`	Reports the result of constraint violations

3.2.3. Main Bean Validation Annotations

Along with APIs, Bean Validation comes with a set of annotations. Table 3 lists a subset of the most commonly used annotations.

Table 3. Main Bean Validation Annotations

Annotation	Description
`@Constraint`	Marks an annotation as being a Bean Validation constraint
`@Email`	The string has to be a well-formed email address
`@Max, @Min`	The annotated element must be a number whose value is lower or equal, or higher or equal to the specified value
`@Null, @NotNull`	The annotated element must be null or not null
`@Past, @Future`	The annotated element must be an instant, date or time in the past or in the future
`@Valid`	Marks a property, method parameter or method return type for validation

This was just a quick introduction of Bean Validation main packages, APIs and annotations. This fascicle will dig into more details in the coming chapters.

3.2.4. Deployment Descriptors

Like several Java technologies, Bean Validation comes with a set of APIs but also some deployment descriptors. A *Deployment Descriptor* (DD) refers to a configuration file that is deployed with the code and configures or overrides parts of the code.

As shown in the diagram in Figure 5, Bean Validation comes with two kinds of XML descriptors:

- `META-INF/validation.xml`: This optional file can be used to customise the configuration of the default `ValidatorFactory`. It can also aggregate zero or many constraint mapping XML descriptors.

- Constraint mapping descriptor: Up to now, we've seen annotations, but Bean Validation also lets you declare constraints via XML. This file describes constraint declarations and closely matches the annotations declaration approach.

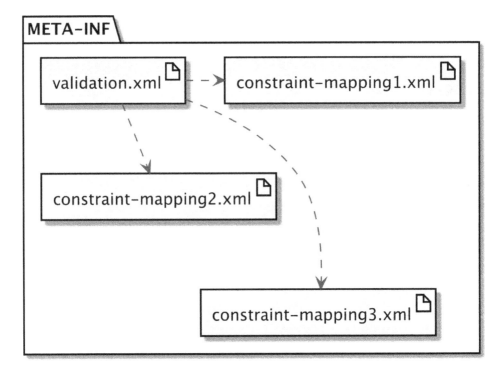

Figure 5. Bean Validation deployment descriptors

Notice that the deployment descriptors are located under the META-INF directory of the application.

Validation

The validation.xml deployment descriptors is optional and is specified in Listing 14.

Listing 14. validation.xml

```
<validation-config>

  <clock-provider/>
  <constraint-mapping/>
  <constraint-validator-factory/>
  <default-provider/>
  <message-interpolator/>
  <parameter-name-provider/>
  <traversable-resolver/>
  <value-extractor/>
  <property name=""/>
</validation-config>
```

The root element of the validation.xml file in Listing 14 is the validation-config element. This element consists of the following sub-elements:

- clock-provider: Represents the fully qualified class name of the ClockProvider implementation.

- constraint-mapping: Represents the resource path of an XML mapping file.

- constraint-validator-factory: Represents the fully qualified class name of the ConstraintValidatorFactory implementation.

- default-provider: Represents the class name of the provider specific ValidationProvider implementation class.

- message-interpolator: Represents the fully qualified class name of the MessageInterpolator implementation.

- parameter-name-provider: represents the fully qualified class name of the ParameterNameProvider implementation

- traversable-resolver: Represents the fully qualified class name of the TraversableResolver implementation.

- value-extractor: Represents the fully qualified class name of a ValueExtractor implementation.

- property: Represents a key/value pair property providing room to provider specific configurations.

Constraint Descriptor

The XML constraint descriptor serves as both an alternative to and an overriding mechanism for constraint annotations. It is optional and only taken into account by the Bean Validation provider if specified on the validation.xml (with the constraint-mapping element). Listing 15 specifies the structure of the constraint descriptor XML file.

Listing 15. Mapping Descriptor

```xml
<constraint-mappings>

  <default-package/>
  <constraint-definition annotation="">
    <validated-by/>
  </constraint-definition>

  <bean class="">
    <class>
      <constraint annotation=""/>
      <group-sequence/>
    </class>
    <field name="">
      <constraint annotation="">
        <message/>
      </constraint>
    </field>
    <constructor/>
    <getter name=""/>
    <method name=""/>
  </bean>
</constraint-mappings>
```

More on constraint descriptors in Chapter 4.

Now that you know the basis of validation, have run a "*Hello World*" example, and know a bit more terminology, let's use the following chapters to dig more into Bean Validation.

[42] Maven https://maven.apache.org

[43] JUnit http://junit.org

[44] Bean Validation GitHub https://github.com/eclipse-ee4j/beanvalidation-api

Chapter 4. Applying Constraints

 The code in this chapter can be found at https://github.com/agoncal/agoncal-fascicle-bean-validation/tree/2.0/applying-constraints

4.1. Built-in Constraints

Bean Validation is a specification that allows you to write your own constraints and validate them. But it also comes with some common built-in constraints. Table 4 gives you an exhaustive list of all the built-in constraints (i.e. all the constraints that you can use out of the box in your code without developing any annotation or implementation class). All of the built-in constraints are defined in the `javax.validation.constraints` package. Being part of the specification, you can use them in a portable way across all the Bean Validation implementations.

Table 4. Exhaustive List of Built-in Constraint Annotations

Constraint	Accepted Types	Description
`@Null`, `@NotNull`	`Object`	The annotated element must be null or not
`@NotBlank`	`CharSequence`	The element must not be null and must contain at least one non-whitespace character
`@NotEmpty`	`CharSequence`, `Collection`, `Map`, arrays	The annotated element must not be null or empty
`@Size`	`CharSequence`, `Collection`, `Map`, arrays	The element size must be between the specified boundaries
`@Max`, `@Min`	`BigDecimal`, `BigInteger`, `byte`, `short`, `int`, `long`, and their wrappers	The element must be greater or lower than the specified value
`@DecimalMax`, `@DecimalMin`	`BigDecimal`, `BigInteger`, `CharSequence`, `byte`, `short`, `int`, `long`, and their respective wrappers	The element must be greater or lower than the specified value
`@Negative`, `@NegativeOrZero`, `@Positive`, `@PositiveOrZero`	`BigDecimal`, `BigInteger`, `byte`, `short`, `int`, `long`, and their wrappers	The element must be negative or positive, including zero or not
`@Digits`	`BigDecimal`, `BigInteger`, `CharSequence`, `byte`, `short`, `int`, `long`, and respective wrappers	The annotated element must be a number within the accepted range
`@AssertFalse`, `@AssertTrue`	`Boolean`, `boolean`	The annotated element must be either false or true

Constraint	Accepted Types	Description
@Future, @FutureOrPresent, @Past, @PastOrPresent	Calendar, Date and types of the Java 8 date and time API (JSR 310)	The annotated element must be a date in the future or in the past, including the present or not
@Email	CharSequence	The string has to be a well-formed email address
@Pattern	CharSequence	The element must match the specified regular expression

4.2. Applying Built-in Constraints

These built-in constraints can be applied to different parts of our code. As an example, Listing 16 shows an Order class that uses constraint annotations on attributes, containers (List), constructors, and business methods.

Listing 16. A POJO Using Constraints on Several Element Types

```
public class Order {

  @NotNull @Pattern(regexp = "[CDM][0-9]+")
  private String orderId;
  @NotNull @Min(1)
  private BigDecimal totalAmount;
  @PastOrPresent
  private Instant creationDate;
  @Future
  private LocalDate deliveryDate;

  @NotNull
  private List<OrderLine> orderLines;

  public Order(@PastOrPresent Instant creationDate) {
    this.creationDate = creationDate;
  }

  @NotNull
  public Double calculateTotalAmount(@Positive Double changeRate) {
    return complexCalculation();
  }

  // Constructors, getters, setters
}
```

As you can see, Bean Validation is flexible enough to apply the same built-in constraints on different element types.

4.2.1. Constraining Attributes

Bean Validation takes its name from the Java Bean design pattern.[45] A Java Bean has properties, getters, setters, and methods. The most common use case of Bean Validation is constraining the attributes of a class. Listing 17 shows a Book class, containing attributes annotated with Bean Validation built-in constraints.

Listing 17. A Book Constraining Its Properties

```java
public class Book {

    @NotNull
    private String title;
    @Digits(integer = 4, fraction = 2)
    private Float price;
    @Size(max = 2000)
    private String description;
    private Integer isbn;
    @Positive
    private Integer nbOfPages;
    @Email
    private String authorEmail;

    // Constructors, getters, setters
}
```

Thanks to Bean Validation, the Book class in Listing 17, adds semantic to its properties. Instead of just saying that the price attribute is a Float, it actually expresses that the price of a book can have 4 numbers and 2 fractions. This is how we can read this code:

- A book must have a title (@NotNull),
- The price of a book must have maximum 4 digits for the number and maximum 2 digits for the fraction,
- The description of the book can be null, and if not, its length cannot be greater than 2000 characters,
- The number of pages must be a positive integer, and
- The author's email must be well-formed if not null. If you need the email to be not null and well-formed, then you need to use both the @NotNull and @Email annotations.

Constraints can also be applied on top of getter methods instead of attributes. The semantics of the code in Listing 17 is the same as Listing 18. You just have to define constraints either on the attribute or on the getter but not on both at the same time. It is best to stay consistent throughout your application code and use annotations always on attributes or always on getters.

Listing 18. A Book Constraining Its Getters

```java
public class Book {

  private String title;
  private Float price;
  private String description;
  private Integer isbn;
  private Integer nbOfPages;
  private String authorEmail;

  @NotNull
  public String getTitle() {
    return title;
  }

  @Digits(integer = 4, fraction = 2)
  public Float getPrice() {
    return price;
  }

  @Size(max = 2000)
  public String getDescription() {
    return description;
  }

  public Integer getIsbn() {
    return isbn;
  }

  @Positive
  public Integer getNbOfPages() {
    return nbOfPages;
  }

  @Email
  public String getAuthorEmail() {
    return authorEmail;
  }

  // Setters
}
```

It's worth mentioning that, when you annotate the getters, the constraints become part of the bean's public API and Javadoc. In some IDEs, the constraint is visible when hovering over the getter for example.

4.2.2. Constraining Containers

We've just seen how to constrain basic data types. But Bean Validation also allows us to add annotations to elements of collections of type Collection, Map, arrays and even custom containers. As you can see in Listing 19, not only can we constrain the container itself (e.g. "Make sure the list of order lines is not empty"), but we can also constrain the contents of the container (e.g. "Make sure that in the list of emails, each item is a valid email").

Listing 19. An Order Applying Built-in Constraints to Containers

```java
public class Order {

    private String orderId;
    private Double totalAmount;

    @NotEmpty
    private List<OrderLine> orderLines;

    @NotEmpty
    private List<@Email @NotBlank String> emails;

    // Constructors, getters, setters
}
```

In Listing 19, we've defined an emails property for an Order class, which contains elements that cannot be a blank String and must be valid email addresses. Note that the @NotEmpty validation applies to the entire collection and not to the String elements. On the contrary, @Email and @NotBlank apply to each element of the collection.

The same behaviour can be used to validate the elements of a Map collection. In Listing 20, we define that a CD album has a number of tracks. The tracks property cannot be null, and we do not allow to having more than five tracks per CD. Each track is made up of a position and a title. The position of the track (e.g. the first, the second or the third track of the album) must be a positive number, while the title of the track is a String which cannot be blank. Notice that we can add validation annotations both for the key and the value of a Map entry.

Listing 20. A Book with Optional Attributes

```java
public class CD {

    @NotNull
    private String title;
    private String musicCompany;

    @NotEmpty @Size(max = 5)
    private Map<@Positive Integer, @NotBlank String> tracks;

    // Constructors, getters, setters
}
```

4.2.3. Constraining Optionals

Optional is another sort of "container". The java.util.Optional class was introduced in Java SE 8. The purpose of this class is to provide a type-level solution for representing optional values instead of using null references. As you see in the code below, the API returns true if and only if the value wrapped is not null.

```
assertTrue(Optional.ofNullable("contains a value").isPresent());
assertFalse(Optional.ofNullable(null).isPresent());
```

Validation constraints can also be applied to an Optional value. In Listing 21, a book can have an optional number of pages as well as an optional author's email.

Listing 21. A Bean with Constraints on Optional

```
public class Book {

  private String title;
  private Integer isbn;
  private Integer nbOfPages;
  private String authorEmail;

  public String getTitle() {
    return title;
  }

  public Integer getIsbn() {
    return isbn;
  }

  public Optional<@Positive Integer> getNbOfPages() {
    return Optional.ofNullable(nbOfPages);
  }

  public Optional<@Email String> getAuthorEmail() {
    return Optional.ofNullable(authorEmail);
  }

  // Setters
}
```

Optional means that if the number of pages or the author's email attributes are null, the bean is still valid. The Optional is there to force you to check if the value is not null before using it (e.g. book.getNbOfPages().isPresent()). But if the value is present, then the number of pages must be positive (@Positive) and the email must be valid (@Email).

4.2.4. Constraining Methods

Method-level constraints were introduced in Bean Validation 1.1. These are constraints declared on methods as well as constructors (getters are not considered constrained methods by default). These constraints can be added to the method parameters (called parameter constraints) or to the method itself (called return value constraints). In this way, Bean Validation can be used to describe and validate the contract applied to a given method or constructor. This enables utilising the well-known *Programming by Contract* paradigm.[16]

* *Preconditions* must be met by the caller before a method or constructor is invoked, and

* *Postconditions* are guaranteed to the caller after a method or constructor invocation returns.

Listing 22 shows how you can use method-level constraints in several ways. The `CardValidator` service validates a credit card through a specific validation algorithm. This algorithm is passed to the constructor and cannot be null. For that, the constructor uses the `@NotNull` constraint on the `ValidationAlgorithm` parameter. Then, the two `validate()` methods return a boolean (indicating the validity of the credit card) with an `@AssertTrue` constraint on the returned type. In our example, this is to ensure the credit card is always valid (postcondition). The `validate()` methods also have some constraints like `@NotNull` and `@Future` on the method parameters to validate input parameters (preconditions).

Listing 22. A Service with Constructor and Method-level Constraints

```java
public class CardValidator {

  private ValidationAlgorithm algorithm;

  public CardValidator(@NotNull ValidationAlgorithm algorithm) {
    this.algorithm = algorithm;
  }

  @AssertTrue
  public Boolean validate(@NotNull CreditCard creditCard) {

    return algorithm.validate(creditCard.getNumber(), creditCard.getControlNumber());
  }

  @AssertTrue
  public Boolean validate(@NotNull String number, @Future Date expiryDate, @NotNull
Integer controlNumber) {

    return algorithm.validate(number, controlNumber);
  }
}
```

4.3. Multiple Constraints for the Same Target

Sometimes it is useful to apply the same constraint more than once on the same target with different properties or groups (more on groups later). A common example is the `@Pattern` constraint, which validates that its target matches a specified regular expression. Listing 23 shows how to apply two regular expressions on the same attribute. Multiple constraints use the AND operator. This means that the orderId attribute needs to follow both regular expressions to be valid.

Listing 23. A POJO Applying Multiple Pattern Constraints on the Same Attribute

```
public class Order {

    @Pattern(regexp = "[CDM][A-Z][0-9]*")
    @Pattern(regexp = ".[A-Z].*?")
    private String orderId;
    private Instant creationDate;
    private Double totalAmount;
    private LocalDate paymentDate;
    private LocalDate deliveryDate;

    // Constructors, getters, setters
}
```

Java SE 8 introduced the java.lang.annotation.Repeatable annotation. It is used to indicate that the annotation type whose declaration it annotates is repeatable. The constraint annotation is defined as an array of itself and this array is marked as Repeatable. In this case, Bean Validation treats constraint arrays in a special way: each element of the array is processed as a regular constraint. Listing 24 shows the @Pattern constraint annotation being Repeatable as well as defining an inner interface (called List) with an element Pattern[]. The inner interface must have the retention RUNTIME and must use the same set of targets as the initial constraint (here METHOD, FIELD, ANNOTATION_TYPE, CONSTRUCTOR, PARAMETER).

Listing 24. The Repeatable Pattern Constraint Defining a List of Patterns

```
@Target({METHOD, FIELD, ANNOTATION_TYPE, CONSTRUCTOR, PARAMETER, TYPE_USE})
@Retention(RUNTIME)
@Repeatable(Pattern.List.class)
@Constraint(validatedBy = {})
public @interface Pattern {

    // ...

    @Target({METHOD, FIELD, ANNOTATION_TYPE, CONSTRUCTOR, PARAMETER, TYPE_USE})
    @Retention(RUNTIME)
    @Documented
    @interface List {
        Pattern[] value();
    }
}
```

If you come across Java SE 7 code, then you might see the old syntax that uses the array of Pattern annotations. Listing 25 has the same meaning as the code in Listing 23 but doesn't use the new Repeatable annotation.

```java
public class Order {

  @Pattern.List({
    @Pattern(regexp = "[CDM][A-Z][0-9]*"),
    @Pattern(regexp = ".[A-Z].*?")
  })
  private String orderId;
  private Instant creationDate;
  private Double totalAmount;
  private LocalDate paymentDate;
  private LocalDate deliveryDate;

  // Constructors, getters, setters
}
```

 When you develop your own constraint annotation, you should add its corresponding Repeatable annotation.

4.4. Messages

When a constraint is violated, an error message is displayed so the user can fix the value. Each built-in annotation has a default error message. These messages are listed in Table 5.

Table 5. Default Error Message of Built-in Constraint Annotations

Constraint	Default Error Message
@AssertFalse	must be false
@AssertTrue	must be true
@DecimalMax	must be less than ${inclusive == true ? 'or equal to ' : ''}{value}
@DecimalMin	must be greater than ${inclusive == true ? 'or equal to ' : ''}{value}
@Digits	numeric value out of bounds (<{integer} digits>.<{fraction} digits> expected)
@Email	must be a well-formed email address
@Future	must be a future date
@FutureOrPresent	must be a date in the present or in the future
@Max	must be less than or equal to {value}
@Min	must be greater than or equal to {value}
@Negative	must be less than 0
@NegativeOrZero	must be less than or equal to 0
@NotBlank	must not be blank
@NotEmpty	must not be empty

Constraint	Default Error Message
@NotNull	must not be null
@Null	must be null
@Past	must be a past date
@PastOrPresent	must be a date in the past or in the present
@Pattern	must match "{regexp}"
@Positive	must be greater than 0
@PositiveOrZero	must be greater than or equal to 0
@Size	size must be between {min} and {max}

4.4.1. Templates

As you can see from Table 5, an error message can be a fixed text (e.g. "must be greater than 0") or can use templates. For example, the annotation @Size has the default message "size must be between {min} and {max}". {min} and {max} are placeholders, and represent the attributes of the @Size annotation. These placeholders are string literals enclosed in {}. They are extracted from the message and evaluated using Expression Language by the Bean Validation runtime. Let's say you have the following constraint:

```
@Size(min = 4, max = 50)
private String title;
```

If the constraint is violated, meaning that if the size of the title attribute is bigger than 50 for example, the error message will be "size must be between 4 and 50".

4.4.2. Overriding Error Messages

Having a default error message with template is good, but sometimes not enough. Let's consider the following recoveryEmail attribute. It is annotated with the built-in @Email constraint. Therefore, if the value is in the wrong format, Bean Validation will automatically set the error message to its default value. This means that the user will get the message "must be a well-formed email address".

```
@Email
private String recoveryEmail;
```

If the default message is not clear or specific enough, it can be overridden every time at declaration time. Each built-in annotation has a message attribute that can take a String. The example below will set the error message to "Recovery email is not a valid email address" if the value is invalid.

```
@Email(message = "Recovery email is not a valid email address")
private String recoveryEmail;
```

And because the error message can be overridden whenever you use the constraint, you might end up with a code that looks like Listing 26. Here, we have a Customer class that uses error messages in several ways. The userId attribute is annotated with @Email, meaning that if the value is not a well-formed email address, the default error message will be used. On the other hand, the recoveryEmail overrides the default error message. Note that for the firstName and age attributes, the default error messages are overridden with messages using placeholders ({min}, {max} and {value}). You can only use the supported place holders for each constraint. Meaning that you can {min} and {max} for the @Size annotation, but not for the @Pattern for example (which has a {regexp} member).

Listing 26. A Customer Class Declaring Several Error Messages

```java
public class Customer {

    @Email
    private String userId;
    @NotNull
    @Size(min = 4, max = 50, message = "First name length should be between {min} and
{max}")
    private String firstName;
    private String lastName;
    @Email(message = "Recovery email is not a valid email address")
    private String recoveryEmail;
    private LocalDate dateOfBirth;
    @Min(value = 18, message = "Customer is too young. Should be older than {value}")
    private Integer age;

    // Constructors, getters, setters
}
```

4.4.3. Resource Bundles

Of course, having fixed error messages (with or without placeholders) in your code can be restrictive. What if you need to internationalize these messages? That's when Bean Validation goes further by allowing you to externalise error messages in resource bundles. By default, the resource bundle is a file named ValidationMessages.properties which has to be in the class path of the application. The file follows the key/value pair format, so this is what you need to write to externalise an error message:

```
org.agoncal.fascicle.Customer.firstName=The customer first name length should be
between {min} and {max}
org.agoncal.fascicle.Customer.recoveryEmail=The recovery email is not a valid email
address
org.agoncal.fascicle.Customer.age=Customer is too young. He/she should be older than
{value}
```

If you need to internationalize these messages into French, you just need to create a property file named ValidationMessages_fr.properties with the following content:

```
org.agoncal.fascicle.Customer.firstName=La taille du prénom doit être comprise entre
{min} et {max}
org.agoncal.fascicle.Customer.recoveryEmail=Le mail de secours doit être valide
org.agoncal.fascicle.Customer.age=Le client est trop jeune. Il doit avoir plus de
{value} ans
```

Using these error messages is quite straightforward. Instead of writing the error message text (e.g. @Email(message = "Recovery email is not a valid email address")) you just add the error message key (e.g. @Email(message = "{org.agoncal.fascicle.Customer.recoveryEmail}")). Based on the key, Bean Validation will then pick up the right error message depending on the locale (English or French). Listing 27 shows how to use error message keys in a POJO.

Listing 27. A Customer Class Using Error Messages Keys

```java
public class Customer {

    @Email
    private String userId;
    @NotNull
    @Size(min = 4, max = 50, message = "{org.agoncal.fascicle.Customer.firstName}")
    private String firstName;
    private String lastName;
    @Email(message = "{org.agoncal.fascicle.Customer.recoveryEmail}")
    private String recoveryEmail;
    private LocalDate dateOfBirth;
    @Min(value = 18, message = "{org.agoncal.fascicle.Customer.age}")
    private Integer age;

    // Constructors, getters, setters
}
```

4.5. Deployment Descriptors

So far, all the code examples use annotations, but Bean Validation also allows you to define constraints using XML under the META-INF directory. For this purpose, validation.xml can be used to refine some of the Bean Validation behaviours such as the default Bean Validation provider, the message interpolator, and some other specific properties. Then, you can define other files (known as constraint mapping files) to describe constraint declarations on your beans. Notice that, by default, the XML declarations override the annotations.

Listing 28 shows the META-INF/validation.xml deployment descriptor that has a <validation-config> XML root element but, more importantly, defines one external constraint mapping file: constraints.xml (Listing 29).

Listing 28. A validation.xml File Declaring a Constraint Mapping File

```xml
<?xml version="1.0" encoding="UTF-8"?>
<validation-config
   xmlns:xsi="http://www.w3.org/2001/XMLSchema-instance"
   xmlns="http://xmlns.jcp.org/xml/ns/validation/configuration"
   xsi:schemaLocation="http://xmlns.jcp.org/xml/ns/validation/configuration
http://xmlns.jcp.org/xml/ns/validation/configuration/validation-configuration-2.0.xsd"
   version="2.0">

   <constraint-mapping>META-INF/constraints.xml</constraint-mapping>

</validation-config>
```

Listing 29. A File Defining Constraints on a Bean

```xml
<?xml version="1.0" encoding="UTF-8"?>
<constraint-mappings
   xmlns:xsi="http://www.w3.org/2001/XMLSchema-instance"
   xmlns="http://xmlns.jcp.org/xml/ns/validation/mapping"
   xsi:schemaLocation="http://xmlns.jcp.org/xml/ns/validation/mapping
http://xmlns.jcp.org/xml/ns/validation/configuration/validation-mapping-2.0.xsd"
   version="2.0">

   <bean class="org.agoncal.fascicle.beanvalidation.applyingconstraints.Book" ignore-
annotations="false">
      <field name="title">
        <constraint annotation="javax.validation.constraints.NotNull">
          <message>Title should not be null</message>
        </constraint>
      </field>
      <field name="price">
        <constraint annotation="javax.validation.constraints.Digits">
          <element name="integer">4</element>
          <element name="fraction">2</element>
        </constraint>
      </field>
      <field name="description">
        <constraint annotation="javax.validation.constraints.Size">
          <element name="max">2000</element>
        </constraint>
      </field>
      <field name="nbOfPages">
        <constraint annotation="javax.validation.constraints.Positive"/>
      </field>
      <field name="authorEmail">
        <constraint annotation="javax.validation.constraints.Email"/>
      </field>
   </bean>
</constraint-mappings>
```

The constraints.xml file in Listing 29 defines the XML metadata for declaring constraints on the Book class. It first applies a @NotNull constraint on the title attribute and redefines the default error message ("Title should not be null"). For the price attribute, the Digits constraint is applied with a number of integers set to 4, and the number of fractions set to 2. This resembles the code in Listing 17 where metadata was defined using annotations. By using the XML deployment descriptor, the Book bean defined in Listing 30 does not need annotations anymore.

Listing 30. A Book Bean with No Constraint Annotations Relying on XML Deployment Descriptor

```
public class Book {

  private String title;
  private Float price;
  private String description;
  private Integer isbn;
  private Integer nbOfPages;
  private String authorEmail;

  // Constructors, getters, setters
}
```

[45] Java Beans http://download.oracle.com/otndocs/jcp/7224-javabeans-1.01-fr-spec-oth-JSpec

[46] Programming by Contract https://en.wikipedia.org/wiki/Design_by_contract

Chapter 5. Validating Constraints

So far, we've been applying constraints on attributes, getters, constructors, method parameters, return values and containers. But for validation to occur on all these element types, you need to use validation APIs.

 The code in this chapter can be found at https://github.com/agoncal/agoncal-fascicle-bean-validation/tree/2.0/validating-constraints

5.1. Validation APIs

The validation runtime uses a small set of APIs to be able to validate constraints (see class diagram in Figure 6):

- The main API is the `javax.validation.Validator` interface. It holds the methods to validate objects and graphs of objects independently of the layer in which it is implemented (presentation layer, business layer, or business model).

- The `ExecutableValidator` interface is used for method and constructor parameters validation, as well as returned value.

- Upon validation failure, a set of `javax.validation.ConstraintViolation` interfaces is returned. This interface exposes the constraint violation context as well as the message describing the violation.

- The `ConstraintViolationException` reports the result of constraint violations.

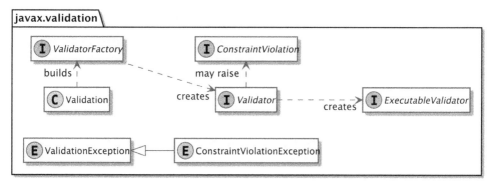

Figure 6. Validation APIs

5.1.1. Validator API

The main entry point for validation is the `Validator` interface. Its API is able to validate instances of beans using only a few methods described in Table 6.

Table 6. Methods of the Validator Interface

Method	Description
`Set<ConstraintViolation<T>> validate()`	Validates all constraints on an object
`Set<ConstraintViolation<T>> validateProperty()`	Validates all constraints placed on a property
`Set<ConstraintViolation<T>> validateValue()`	Validates all constraints placed on a property for a given value
`ExecutableValidator forExecutables()`	Returns a delegate for validating parameters and return values on methods and constructors

The methods `validate()`, `validateProperty()`, and `validateValue()` are used, respectively, for validating an entire bean, a property, or a property for a given value. All methods take a varargs parameter that can be used to specify the constraint groups to validate (as you'll see in Chapter 7).

5.1.2. ConstraintViolation API

All the validating methods listed in Table 6 return a set of `ConstraintViolation` objects which can be iterated in order to see which validation errors occurred. If the set is empty then it means all the constraints are met and the validation has been successful. Otherwise, a `ConstraintViolation` instance is added to the set for each violated constraint. The `ConstraintViolation` describes a single constraint failure and its API gives a lot of useful information about the cause of the failure. Table 7 gives an overview of this API.

Table 7. Methods of the ConstraintViolation Interface

Method	Description
`String getMessage()`	Returns the interpolated error message for this constraint violation
`String getMessageTemplate()`	Returns the non-interpolated error message
`T getRootBean()`	Returns the root bean being validated (handy when cascading validation)
`Class<T> getRootBeanClass()`	Returns the class of the root bean being validated
`Object getLeafBean()`	Returns the leaf bean the constraint is applied on (handy when cascading validation)
`Path getPropertyPath()`	Returns the property path to the value from the root bean
`Object getInvalidValue()`	Returns the value failing to pass the constraint
`ConstraintDescriptor<?> getConstraintDescriptor()`	Returns the constraint metadata
`Object[] getExecutableParameters()`	Returns the constructor or method invocation arguments
`Object getExecutableReturnValue()`	Returns the return value of the constructor or method invocation

5.1.3. Obtaining a Validator

The first step towards validating a bean, a property or a method, is to get hold of a `Validator` instance. You can either get a Validator programmatically (if your code is executed outside a container) or get it injected (if your code is executed inside a container).

If you do it programmatically you need to start with the Validation class which bootstraps the Bean Validation provider. Its buildDefaultValidatorFactory() method builds and returns a ValidatorFactory which in turn is used to build a Validator. The code looks like the following:

```
ValidatorFactory factory = Validation.buildDefaultValidatorFactory();
Validator validator = factory.getValidator();
```

If you need to customise the ValidatorFactory, for example, by using a different provider (here Hibernate Validator), you can also do it as follows:

```
ValidatorFactory factory =
    Validation.byProvider(HibernateValidator.class)
            .configure()
            .buildValidatorFactory();
Validator validator = factory.getValidator();
```

Then you need to manage the life cycle of the ValidatorFactory by yourself and programmatically close it.

```
factory.close();
```

If your code runs on a container allowing the injection via @Inject (Java EE or Spring container), you can inject both the ValidatorFactory and Validator with a single annotation

```
@Inject ValidatorFactory validatorFactory;
@Inject Validator validator;
```

The container looks after the life cycle of the factory. So, you do not need to manually create or close the ValidatorFactory.

 Obtaining a Validator is something that you'll rarely do. Instead it will be done automatically for you at the right point in time of the object life cycle by integrating technologies (e.g. by JPA before persisting data to the database, by JAX-RS when processing an HTTP request etc.). This will be covered in Chapter 8.

5.2. Validating Beans

Once the Validator is obtained programmatically or by injection, we can use its methods to validate either an entire bean or just a single property. Listing 31 shows a CD class with constraints set on properties, on method parameters and return values.

Listing 31. A Bean with Property and Method Constraints

```java
public class CD {

  @NotNull @Size(min = 4, max = 50)
  private String title;
  @NotNull @Positive
  private Float price;
  @Size(min = 10, max = 5000)
  private String description;
  @Pattern(regexp = "[A-Z][a-z]+")
  private String musicCompany;
  @Max(value = 5)
  private Integer numberOfCDs;
  private Float totalDuration;

  @NotNull @DecimalMin("5.8")
  public Float calculatePrice(@DecimalMin("1.4") Float discountRate) {
    return price * discountRate;
  }

  @DecimalMin("9.99")
  public Float calculateVAT() {
    return price * 0.196f;
  }
}
```

To validate all the bean properties, we just need to create an instance of CD and call the Validator.validate() method (see Listing 32). If the instance is valid, then an empty set of ConstraintViolation is returned. The following code validates a CD instance which has a valid title and price. The code then checks that the set of constraint violations is empty.

Listing 32. Validating a Valid Bean

```java
CD cd = new CD().title("Kind of Blue").price(12.5f);

Set<ConstraintViolation<CD>> violations = validator.validate(cd);
assertEquals(0, violations.size());
```

On the other hand, the code in Listing 33 will return two ConstraintViolation objects - one for the title and another one for the price (both violating @NotNull):

Listing 33. Validating an Invalid Bean

```java
CD cd = new CD();

Set<ConstraintViolation<CD>> violations = validator.validate(cd);
assertEquals(2, violations.size());
```

In Listing 34, we create a CD with a negative price. You can see how we use the ConstraintViolation API. When testing the values of our CD, we can check the error message, the message template, the invalid value, or the property.

Listing 34. Checking the ConstraintViolation API

```
CD cd = new CD().title("Kind of Blue").price(-10f);

Set<ConstraintViolation<CD>> violations = validator.validate(cd);
assertEquals(1, violations.size());
ConstraintViolation<CD> violation = violations.iterator().next();

assertEquals("must be greater than 0", violation.getMessage());
assertEquals("{javax.validation.constraints.Positive.message}", violation
.getMessageTemplate());
assertEquals(-10f, violation.getInvalidValue());
assertEquals("price", violation.getPropertyPath().toString());
assertEquals(CD.class, violation.getRootBeanClass());
assertTrue(violation.getConstraintDescriptor().getAnnotation() instanceof javax
.validation.constraints.Positive);
assertEquals("Kind of Blue", violation.getRootBean().getTitle());
```

5.3. Validating Properties

So far, we have seen how to validate the entire bean in the previous examples. But with the help of the Validator.validateProperty() method, we can also validate a single named property of a given bean. This method is useful for partial object validation.

The code in Listing 35 creates a CD object with a null title and a null price, meaning that the bean is not valid. But because we only validate the numberOfCDs property, the validation succeeds and the set of constraint violations is empty.

Listing 35. Validating Valid Properties

```
CD cd = new CD().numberOfCDs(2);

Set<ConstraintViolation<CD>> violations = validator.validateProperty(cd, "numberOfCDs
");
assertEquals(0, violations.size());
```

On the contrary, the code in Listing 36 raises one constraint violation because the maximum number of CDs should be 5 and not 7. Notice that we use the ConstraintViolation API to check the interpolated message returned by the violation, the invalid value, and the message template.

Listing 36. Validating Invalid Properties

```
CD cd = new CD().numberOfCDs(7);

Set<ConstraintViolation<CD>> violations = validator.validateProperty(cd, "numberOfCDs
");

assertEquals(1, violations.size());
ConstraintViolation<CD> violation = violations.iterator().next();

assertEquals("must be less than or equal to 5", violation.getMessage());
assertEquals(7, violation.getInvalidValue());
assertEquals("{javax.validation.constraints.Max.message}", violation
.getMessageTemplate());
```

5.4. Validating Values

Using the `Validator.validateValue()` method, you can check whether a single property of a given class can be validated successfully, if the property has the specified value. This method is useful for ahead-of-time validation because you don't even have to create an instance of the bean and populate its values. This for instance is very practical for validating user input into the controls of a UI before actually populating a model with these values.

The code in Listing 37 doesn't create a CD object but just refers to the `numberOfCDs` attribute of the CD class. It passes a value and checks if the property is valid (number of CDs lower than or equal to 5) or not.

Listing 37. Validating Values

```
violations = validator.validateValue(CD.class, "numberOfCDs", 2);
assertEquals(0, violations.size());

violations = validator.validateValue(CD.class, "numberOfCDs", 7);
assertEquals(1, violations.size());
```

5.5. Validating Methods

So far we've seen how to use the `Validator` interface to validate attributes, properties and values. Since Bean Validation 1.1, we can also validate methods and constructors.

5.5.1. ExecutableValidator API

Table 6 defines the methods found in the `Validator` interface. The API to validate method parameters, constructor parameters and return values can be found on the interface `javax.validation.ExecutableValidator`. The `Validator.forExecutables()` method returns an `ExecutableValidator` on which you can invoke `validateParameters()`, `validateReturnValue()`, `validateConstructorParameters()`, or `validateConstructorReturnValue()`. Table 8 describes the

Table 8. Methods of the ExecutableValidator Interface

Method	Description
Set<ConstraintViolation<T>> validateParameters()	Validates all constraints placed on the parameters of a method
Set<ConstraintViolation<T>> validateReturnValue()	Validates all return value constraints of a method
Set<ConstraintViolation<T>> validateConstructorParameters()	Validates all constraints placed on the parameters of a constructor
Set<ConstraintViolation<T>> validateConstructorReturnValue()	Validates all return value constraints of a constructor

5.5.2. Validating Method Parameters

Let's see how to use the ExecutableValidator interface to validate method parameters. In Listing 38 the CD bean has a method to calculate the price of a CD album. This method takes a parameter representing the discount rate and multiplies it by the price. As you can see, the @DecimalMin annotation constrains the value of this parameter, as it cannot be less than 1.4.

Listing 38. A Bean with Method Constraints

```java
public class CD {

  @NotNull @DecimalMin("5.8")
  public Float calculatePrice(@DecimalMin("1.4") Float discountRate) {
    return price * discountRate;
  }

}
```

The code in Listing 39 calls the calculatePrice() method passing the value 1.2. This will cause a constraint violation on the parameter as it violates @DecimalMin("1.4") constraint. To do this, we need to create a java.lang.reflect.Method object targeting the calculatePrice() method with a parameter of type Float. Then we invoke the validateParameters() method on ExecutableValidator passing the bean (CD object), the method to invoke (calculatePrice() method), and the parameter value (here 1.2). The final assert should then check that a constraint has been violated.

```
CD cd = new CD().title("Kind of Blue").price(12.5f);

ExecutableValidator methodValidator = validator.forExecutables();
Method method = CD.class.getMethod("calculatePrice", Float.class);
Set<ConstraintViolation<CD>> violations = methodValidator.validateParameters(cd,
method, new Object[]{new Float(1.2)});
assertEquals(1, violations.size());
```

 Chapter 8 focuses on integrating Bean Validation with other technologies. You will see that validating method parameters is automatically done in JAX-RS, for example. You don't need to programmatically do it.

5.6. Cascading Validation

By default, if one bean (e.g. Order) has a reference to another bean (e.g. Address), or to a list of beans (e.g. List<OrderLine>), the validation is not transitive to nested beans. In addition to supporting instance validation, validation of graphs of objects is also supported. In other words, validating one bean is a good start, but often, beans are nested one into another. To validate a graph of beans in one go, we can apply cascading validation with the @Valid annotation. @Valid marks a property, method parameter or method return type to be included for cascading validation. This feature is also referred to as object graph validation.

In Listing 40, the Order bean uses a few Bean Validation annotations: order identifier must not be null, delivery address must be valid, and the list of ordered items must be valid too.

Listing 40. Order Cascading Validation to Its Order Lines

```
public class Order {

  @NotNull
  private Long id;
  private Double totalAmount;
  @NotNull @Valid
  private Address deliveryAddress;
  private List<@Valid OrderLine> orderLines;

  // Constructors, getters, setters
}
```

In Listing 40, the @Valid constraint will instruct Bean Validator to delve into the Address and OrderLine, and validate all constraints found there. This means that each order line must have a positive unitPrice and a positive quantity (see Listing 41).

Listing 41. OrderLine Has Its Own Constraints

```java
public class OrderLine {

  private String item;
  @NotNull @PositiveOrZero
  private Double unitPrice;
  @NotNull @Positive
  private Integer quantity;

  // Constructors, getters, setters
}
```

To be valid, an address has a mandatory street, city and zipcode (see Listing 42).

Listing 42. Address Has Its Own Constraints

```java
public class Address {

  @NotNull
  private String street;
  @NotNull
  private String city;
  @NotNull @Size(max = 5)
  private String zipcode;

  // Constructors, getters, setters
}
```

Listing 43 shows how to validate an order. As you can see, there is nothing special to be done here. We just create the object graph with one purchase order containing two order lines, and use the `validator.validate(order)` method as usual. Bean Validation will automatically cascade the validation to the delivery address and the two order lines.

Listing 43. Validating an Order with Valid OrderLines

```java
Order order = new Order().id(1234L).totalAmount(40.5);
order.setDeliveryAddress(new Address().street("Ritherdon Rd").zipcode("SE123").city(
"London"));
order.add(new OrderLine().item("Help").quantity(1).unitPrice(10.5));
order.add(new OrderLine().item("Sergeant Pepper").quantity(2).unitPrice(15d));

Set<ConstraintViolation<Order>> violations = validator.validate(order);
displayConstraintViolations(violations);
assertEquals(0, violations.size());
```

In Listing 44, we are purposely supplying an invalid value to the `OrderLine` (quantity(null)) to see the `@Valid` annotation in action. Notice how we use the `getRootBean()` and `getLeafBean()` methods. They respectively give us access to the `Order` bean (the root) and the `OrderLine` bean (the leaf). The method `getPropertyPath()` gives us the exact location of the constraint violation: the attribute `quantity` of the first order line in the array (`orderLines[0].quantity`).

Listing 44. First OrderLine Has Null Quantity Therefore Order Is Invalid

```
Order order = new Order().id(1234L).totalAmount(40.5);
order.setDeliveryAddress(new Address().street("Ritherdon Rd").zipcode("SE123").city(
"London"));
order.add(new OrderLine().item("Help").quantity(null).unitPrice(10.5));
order.add(new OrderLine().item("Sergeant Pepper").quantity(2).unitPrice(15d));

Set<ConstraintViolation<Order>> violations = validator.validate(order);
assertEquals(1, violations.size());
ConstraintViolation<Order> violation = violations.iterator().next();

assertEquals("orderLines[0].quantity", violation.getPropertyPath().toString());
assertEquals(Order.class, violation.getRootBean().getClass());
assertEquals(OrderLine.class, violation.getLeafBean().getClass());
```

If we remove the `@Valid` annotation from the `orderLines` attributes in Listing 40, then the code in Listing 44 will not validate the null value on `quantity`; no constraint will be violated, therefore the `order` bean will be considered valid.

But `@Valid` can be used in other different ways. The example below will first cascade the validation on `Order` and will only invoke the `sendPurchaseOrder()` method if the order is valid.

```
public String sendPurchaseOrder(@Valid Order order)
```

`@Valid` can also be used on containers. In the example below, we cascade validation on the `Map` keys and values:

```
Map<@Valid Customer, @Valid Order> ordersForCustomers
```

Chapter 6. Writing Constraints

You know how to use Bean Validation to apply built-in constraints on beans and how to validate them. But the beauty of Bean Validation is that it comes with a set of APIs allowing you to create your own constraints. This can be very useful when your business needs specific constraints (e.g. ISBN number format, URL format etc.). Just create your own, and reuse them anywhere.

Note that some Bean Validation implementations, as well as other contributors, have created their own set of constraints. For example, Hibernate Validator has @CreditCardNumber, @Currency, @ISBN, @Range, @SafeHtml or @URL that can be handy for your projects.[17]

 The code in this chapter can be found at https://github.com/agoncal/agoncal-fascicle-bean-validation/tree/2.0/writing-constraints

6.1. Constraint Definition APIs

Today, Java developers are used to annotations that have flourished throughout our code (e.g. @Entity, @Service, @Transactional, @Path etc.). With Bean Validation, developers can write their own annotations that will define their own made constraints.

In fact, Bean Validation constraints are defined by the combination of:

- An annotation (see Listing 45) defining the constraint (e.g. @Size). This annotation has to be itself (meta-)annotated with @Constraint, and can then be applied on types, methods, fields, or other constraint annotations in the case of composition (more on constraint composition in the sections that follow).

- A class, or classes, implementing the algorithm of the constraint (see Listing 46) with a given type (e.g. String, Integer, MyBean). This class must implement the ConstraintValidator interface. While the annotation expresses the constraint on the domain model, the validation implementation decides whether a given value passes the constraint or not.

- ValidationException that can be thrown if the constraint definition is wrong (e.g. ConstraintDeclarationException, ConstraintDefinitionException, MessageDescriptorFormatException etc.). When you develop your own business constraints, you usually don't have to handle these exceptions.

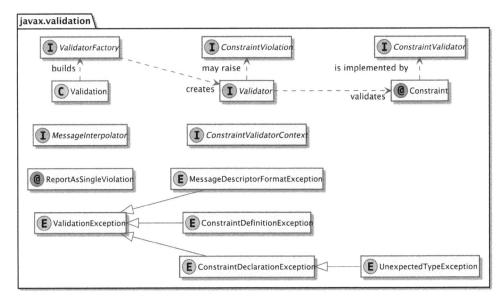

Figure 7. Constraint definition APIs

6.1.1. Constraint Annotation

A constraint on a JavaBean is expressed through one annotation. An annotation is considered a constraint if its retention policy contains RUNTIME and if the annotation itself is annotated with javax.validation.Constraint (which refers to its list of constraint validation implementations). Listing 45 shows the Size constraint annotation.

Listing 45. The Size Constraint Annotation

```java
@Target({METHOD, FIELD, ANNOTATION_TYPE, CONSTRUCTOR, PARAMETER, TYPE_USE})
@Retention(RUNTIME)
@Constraint(validatedBy = {})
@Repeatable(Size.List.class)
@Documented
public @interface Size {

    String message() default "{javax.validation.constraints.Size.message}";
    Class<?>[] groups() default {};
    Class<? extends Payload>[] payload() default {};

    int min() default 0;
    int max() default Integer.MAX_VALUE;

    @Target({METHOD, FIELD, ANNOTATION_TYPE, CONSTRUCTOR, PARAMETER, TYPE_USE})
    @Retention(RUNTIME)
    @Documented
    @interface List {
        Size[] value();
    }
}
```

Constraint annotations are just regular annotations, so they must define some meta-annotations.

- @Target({METHOD, FIELD etc.}): Specifies the target to which the annotation can be used (more on this next).

- @Retention(RUNTIME): Specifies how the annotation will be operated. It is mandatory to use RUNTIME to allow the provider (the Bean Validation implementation) to inspect your objects at runtime.

- @Constraint(validatedBy = {}): Specifies the class (one or a list of classes) that encapsulates the validation algorithm.

- @Repeatable: References the corresponding List annotation. This marks the constraint annotation type as repeatable and lets the developer specify the constraint several times on the same element.

- @Documented: This optional meta-annotation specifies if this annotation will be included in the Javadoc.

Moreover, the Bean Validation specification requires each constraint annotation to define three extra attributes to these meta-annotations.

- message: This attribute (which is generally defaulted to a key) provides the ability for the constraint to return an internationalized error message if the constraint is not valid.

- groups: Groups are typically used to control the order in which constraints are evaluated, or to perform partial validation.

- payload: This attribute is used to associate metadata information with a constraint.

Once your constraint defines all the mandatory meta-annotations and elements, you can add any specific parameter you need. For example, the constraint @Size that validates the size of a String uses two attributes named min and max specifying the minimum and maximum length of a String.

Target

When you create a new constraint, you need to decide on which element types (attribute, getter etc.) it can be used. This is a design decision that developers have to make and it is implemented using the @Target(ElementType.*) meta-annotation (see Listing 45).

- FIELD for constrained attributes,
- METHOD for constrained getters, method return values, and cross-parameters,
- CONSTRUCTOR for constrained constructor return values,
- PARAMETER for constrained method and constructor parameters,
- TYPE_USE for container element constraints,
- TYPE for constrained beans, interfaces and superclasses, and
- ANNOTATION_TYPE for constraints composing other constraints.

As you can see, constraint annotations can be applied to most of the element types defined in Java. Only static fields and static methods cannot be validated by Bean Validation.

6.1.2. ConstraintValidator

Constraints are defined by the combination of an annotation and zero or more implementation classes. The implementation classes are specified by the validatedBy element of @Constraint. Listing 46 shows the implementation class for the @Size annotation on Strings (CharSequence).

Listing 46. The Size Constraint Implementation for CharSequence

```java
public class SizeValidatorForCharSequence implements ConstraintValidator<Size,
CharSequence> {
  private int min;
  private int max;

  @Override
  public void initialize(Size parameters) {
    this.min = parameters.min();
    this.max = parameters.max();
  }

  @Override
  public boolean isValid(CharSequence charSequence, ConstraintValidatorContext ctx) {
    if (charSequence == null) {
      return true;
    } else {
      int length = charSequence.length();
      return length >= this.min && length <= this.max;
    }
  }
}
```

As you can see, it implements the `ConstraintValidator` (see Listing 47), binding the interface's type parameters to `Size` (the targeted constraint annotation type) and `CharSequence` (the validated data type).

Listing 47. The ConstraintValidator Interface

```java
public interface ConstraintValidator<A extends Annotation, T> {

  default void initialize(A constraintAnnotation) { }

  boolean isValid(T value, ConstraintValidatorContext context);
}
```

The `ConstraintValidator` interface (see Listing 47) defines two methods that can be implemented by the concrete classes.

- `initialize()`: This default method is called by the Bean Validation provider prior to any use of the constraint. This is where you usually initialise the validator properties from constraint attributes (if any). As part of initialisation, you can also check if constraint attributes are properly set (e.g. `min` attribute on `@Size` is not a negative number) and throw `ValidationException` if not.

- `isValid`: This is where the validation algorithm is implemented. This method is evaluated by the Bean Validation provider each time a given value is validated. It returns false if the value is not valid or true otherwise. The `ConstraintValidatorContext` object carries information and operations available in which context the constraint is validated (as you'll see later).

A constraint implementation performs the validation of a given annotation for a given type. In Listing 46, the @Size constraint is typed to a CharSequence (which means that this constraint can be used on String, CharBuffer, StringBuffer etc.). But you can have a constraint annotation that has different validation algorithms depending on the data type. For example, you could check the size for a String, but also the size for an array, or the size of a Map. In the code that follows, notice that you have several implementations for the same annotation (@Size) but for different data types (Object[], CharSequence, Collection<?> etc.):

```
public class SizeValidatorForArray implements ConstraintValidator<Size, Object[]>
public class SizeValidatorForMap implements ConstraintValidator<Size, Map<?, ?>>
public class SizeValidatorForCharSequence implements ConstraintValidator<Size,
CharSequence>
public class SizeValidatorForCollection implements ConstraintValidator<Size,
Collection<?>>
```

Of course, each implementation uses a different algorithm to validate its data type. For example, the isValid() method of the SizeValidatorForCharSequence below checks the charSequence.length().

```
@Override
public boolean isValid(CharSequence charSequence, ConstraintValidatorContext ctx) {
  if (charSequence == null) {
    return true;
  } else {
    int length = charSequence.length();
    return length >= this.min && length <= this.max;
  }
```

On the other hand, the isValid() method of the SizeValidatorForArray class just checks the length of the array (array.length).

```
@Override
public boolean isValid(Object[] array, ConstraintValidatorContext ctx) {
  if (array == null) {
    return true;
  } else {
    return array.length >= this.min && array.length <= this.max;
  }
}
```

6.1.3. Validator

As we've seen earlier, the main entry point for validation is the Validator interface. Its validation methods go through the following steps for each constraint declaration:

- Determine the appropriate ConstraintValidator implementation to use for the constraint declaration (e.g. determine the SizeValidatorForCharSequence for the @Size constraint on a

String).

- Initialise the constraint parameters if any.
- Execute the isValid() method.
- If isValid returns true, continue to the next constraint.
- If isValid returns false, the Bean Validation provider adds a ConstraintViolation to the list of constraint violations.

If some unrecoverable failure happens during this validation routine, it raises a ValidationException. This exception can be specialised in some situations (invalid group definition, invalid constraint definition, invalid constraint declaration).

6.2. Defining Your Own Constraints

As you've seen so far, the Bean Validation API provides standard built-in constraints, but they cannot meet all your application's needs. Therefore, the API allows you to develop and use your own business constraints. There are several ways to create your own constraints (from aggregating existing constraints to writing one from scratch) and also different styles (generic or class-level).

6.2.1. Constraint Composition

An easy way to create new constraints is by aggregating already existing ones without having an implementation class. This is pretty easy to do if the existing constraints have a @Target(ElementType.ANNOTATION_TYPE), which means that an annotation can be applied on another annotation. This is called constraint composition and allows you to create higher-level constraints.

For Vintage Store, the books must have an ISBN number, and this number needs to follow a specific format to be valid. Thanks to Bean Validation, such a requirement can be implemented using built-in constraints. Listing 48 shows how to create an Isbn constraint just by aggregating built-in constraints from the Bean Validation API.

Listing 48. An Isbn Constraint Aggregating Other Constraints

```java
@Constraint(validatedBy = {})

@NotNull
@Size(min = 7)
@Pattern(regexp = "[a-f]{1,}")
@ReportAsSingleViolation

@Retention(RUNTIME)
@Target({METHOD, FIELD, PARAMETER, TYPE, ANNOTATION_TYPE, CONSTRUCTOR})
@Documented
public @interface Isbn {

    String message() default "Invalid ISBN number";

    Class<?>[] groups() default {};

    Class<? extends Payload>[] payload() default {};
}
```

This Isbn constraint needs to make sure that the ISBN number is not null (@NotNull), the minimum size is seven characters (@Size(min = 7)) and that it follows a complex regular expression (@Pattern). A composed constraint also has to define the message, groups, and payload attributes. Note that there is no implementation class (validatedBy = {}).

Each built-in constraint (@NotNull, @Size, and @Pattern) already has its own error message (the message() element). This means that if you have a null ISBN, the Isbn constraint in Listing 48 will throw the @NotNull error message upon validation instead of the one defined ("Invalid ISBN number"). You may want to have a single error message for the Isbn constraints rather than having several. For that, you could add the @ReportAsSingleViolation annotation. If you do so, the evaluation of the composing constraints stops at the first failing constraint and the error report corresponding to the composed constraint (here, the @Isbn constraint) is generated and returned.

Once this Isbn constraint is defined, the way to use it is straightforward: just annotate the needed attribute, parameter or return value and you are done (see Listing 49).

Listing 49. The Isbn Constraint Used on a Bean

```java
public class Book {

    private String title;
    private Float price;
    @Isbn
    private String isbn;
    private Integer nbOfPages;

    // Constructors, getters, setters
}
```

Constraint composition is useful because it avoids code duplication and facilitates the reuse of more primitive constraints. It is good practice to create simple, generic constraints and use them as building-blocks for more specific, composed constraints as needed.

 When you create a new constraint, make sure you give it a meaningful name. A carefully chosen annotation name will make constraints more readable in the code. You should also check in the implementation you've chosen (e.g. Hibernate Validator) if additional constraints are defined.

6.2.2. Generic Constraint

Simple constraint composition is good practice but is usually not enough. Often you need to have more complex validation algorithms that are specific to your business logic; check a value in a database, delegate some validations to helper classes, and so on. That's when you need to add an implementation class to your constraint annotation.

Listing 50 shows a POJO that represents a network connection to the Vintage Store items server. This POJO has several attributes of type String, each representing a different URL. You want each URL to have a valid format, and even have a specific protocol (e.g. http, ftp etc.), host, and/or port number. The custom @URL constraint makes sure the different String attributes of the ItemServerConnection class respect the URL format. For example, the resourceURL attribute can be any kind of valid URL (e.g. file://www.vintage-shop.com/item/123). On the other hand, you want to constrain the itemURL attribute to have an http protocol and a host name starting with www.vintage-shop.com (e.g. http://www.vintage-shop.com/book/h2g2).

Listing 50. A URL Constraint Annotation Used on Several Attributes

```java
public class ItemServerConnection {

    @URL
    private String resourceURL;
    @NotNull
    @URL(protocol = "http", host = "www.cdbookstore.com")
    private String itemURL;
    @URL(protocol = "ftp", port = 21)
    private String ftpServerURL;
    private Instant lastConnectionDate;

    // Constructors, getters, setters
}
```

The first thing to do to create such a custom URL constraint is to define an annotation. Listing 51 shows the annotation that follows all the Bean Validation pre-requisites (@Constraint meta-annotation, message, groups, and payload attributes) but also adds specific members: protocol, host, and port. These members can then take a value (e.g. @URL(protocol = "http")). A constraint may use any members of any allowed data type. Also note that these attributes have default values such as an empty String for the protocol or -1 for the port number.

Listing 51. The URL Constraint Annotation

```
@Target({METHOD, FIELD, ANNOTATION_TYPE, CONSTRUCTOR, PARAMETER, TYPE_USE})
@Retention(RUNTIME)
@Constraint(validatedBy = {URLValidator.class})
@Repeatable(URL.List.class)
@Documented
public @interface URL {

  String message() default "Malformed URL";
  Class<?>[] groups() default {};
  Class<? extends Payload>[] payload() default {};

  String protocol() default "";
  String host() default "";
  int port() default -1;

  @Target({METHOD, FIELD, ANNOTATION_TYPE, CONSTRUCTOR, PARAMETER, TYPE_USE})
  @Retention(RUNTIME)
  @Documented
  @interface List {
    URL[] value();
  }
}
```

Listing 51 could have aggregated already existing constraints such as @NotNull. But the main difference between a constraint composition and a generic constraint is that it has an implementation class declared in the validatedBy attribute (here it refers to URLValidator.class).

Listing 52 shows the URLValidator implementation class. As you can see it implements the ConstraintValidator interface and therefore the initialize() and isValid() methods. The important thing to note is that URLValidator has the three attributes defined in the annotation (protocol, host, and port) and initialises them in the initialize(URL url) method. This method is invoked when the validator is instantiated. It receives the constraint annotation (here URL) as a parameter so it can extract the values to be used for validation (e.g. the value for the itemURL protocol attribute in Listing 50 is the String "http").

Listing 52. The URL Constraint Implementation

```java
public class URLValidator implements ConstraintValidator<URL, String> {

  private String protocol;
  private String host;
  private int port;

  @Override
  public void initialize(URL url) {
    this.protocol = url.protocol();
    this.host = url.host();
    this.port = url.port();
  }

  @Override
  public boolean isValid(String value, ConstraintValidatorContext ctx) {
    if (value == null || value.length() == 0) {
      return true;
    }

    java.net.URL url;
    try {
      url = new java.net.URL(value);
    } catch (MalformedURLException e) {
      return false;
    }

    if (protocol != null && protocol.length() > 0 && !url.getProtocol().equals
(protocol)) {
      return false;
    }

    if (host != null && host.length() > 0 && !url.getHost().startsWith(host)) {
      return false;
    }

    if (port != -1 && url.getPort() != port) {
      return false;
    }

    return true;
  }
}
```

The isValid() method implements the URL validation algorithm shown in Listing 52. The value
parameter contains the value of the object to validate (e.g. file://www.vintage-shop.com/item/123).
The context parameter encapsulates information about the context in which the validation is being
done (more on that later). The return value is a boolean indicating whether the validation was
successful or not.

The main task of the validation algorithm in Listing 52 is to cast the passed value to a java.net.URL to see if the URL is malformed or not. Then, the method checks that the protocol, host, and port attributes are valid too. If one of these attributes is not valid then false is returned. As you'll see later in the "Validating Constraints" chapter, the Bean Validation provider will use this boolean to create a collection of ConstraintViolation objects.

Note that the isValid() method considers null as a valid value (if (value == null ⋯ return true)). The Bean Validation specification recommends it as good practice to consider null as valid. This way, you do not duplicate the code of the @NotNull constraint. You would have to use both @URL and @NotNull constraints to express that you want a value to represent a valid URL that is not null (such as the itemURL attribute in Listing 50).

The class signature defines the data type to which the constraint is associated. In Listing 52, the URLValidator is implemented for the type String (ConstraintValidator<URL, String>). It means that if you apply the @URL constraint to a different type (e.g. to the lastConnectionDate attribute) you will get a javax.validation.UnexpectedTypeException at validation time because no validator could be found for type java.time.Instant. If you need a constraint to be applied to several data types, you either need to use superclasses where possible (e.g. we could have defined the URLValidator for a CharSequence instead of a String by writing ConstraintValidator<URL, CharSequence>) or need to have several ConstraintValidator implementations (one for String, CharBuffer, StringBuffer, StringBuilder etc.) if the validation algorithm is different.

6.3. ConstraintValidator Context

So far you've seen that constraint implementation classes need to implement ConstraintValidator to define their own isValid() method. The isValid() method signature takes the object to which the constraint is applied but also a ConstraintValidatorContext. This interface encapsulates data related to the context in which the validation is executed by the Bean Validation provider. Table 9 lists the methods defined in javax.validation.ConstraintValidatorContext interface.

Table 9. Methods of the ConstraintValidatorContext Interface

Method	Description
buildConstraintViolationWithTemplate( )	Returns a ConstraintViolationBuilder to allow the building of a custom violation report
disableDefaultConstraintViolation()	Disable the default ConstraintViolation object generation
getDefaultConstraintMessageTemplate()	Returns the current uninterpolated default message
getClockProvider()	Returns the provider for obtaining the current time in the form of a java.time.Clock

The ConstraintValidatorContext interface allows redefinition of the default constraint message. The buildConstraintViolationWithTemplate() method returns a ConstraintViolationBuilder, based on the fluent API pattern, to allow building custom violation reports. The code that follows adds a new constraint violation to the report:

```
context.buildConstraintViolationWithTemplate("Invalid protocol")
      .addConstraintViolation();
```

This technique allows you to generate and create one or more custom report messages. If we take the example of the @URL constraint (Listing 51), we notice that there is only one error message for the entire constraint ("Malformed URL"). But this constraint has several attributes (protocol, host, and port) and we might want to have specific error messages for each attribute such as "Invalid protocol" or "Invalid host."

Listing 53 revisits the URL constraint implementation and uses the ConstraintValidatorContext to change the error message. The code completely disables the default error message generation (disableDefaultConstraintViolation) and solely defines custom error messages for each attribute.

```
public boolean isValid(String value, ConstraintValidatorContext context) {
  if (value == null || value.length() == 0) {
    return true;
  }

  java.net.URL url;
  try {
    url = new java.net.URL(value);
  } catch (MalformedURLException e) {
    return false;
  }

  if (protocol != null && protocol.length() > 0 && !url.getProtocol().equals(protocol
)) {
    context.disableDefaultConstraintViolation();
    context.buildConstraintViolationWithTemplate("Invalid protocol")
.addConstraintViolation();
    return false;
  }

  if (host != null && host.length() > 0 && !url.getHost().startsWith(host)) {
    context.disableDefaultConstraintViolation();
    context.buildConstraintViolationWithTemplate("Invalid host")
.addConstraintViolation();
    return false;
  }

  if (port != -1 && url.getPort() != port) {
    context.disableDefaultConstraintViolation();
    context.buildConstraintViolationWithTemplate("Invalid port")
.addConstraintViolation();
    return false;
  }

  return true;
}
```

6.4. Messages

As seen earlier (Listing 45), a constraint annotation definition has several mandatory attributes: message, groups, and payload. Every constraint must define a default message of type String which is used to create the error message if there is a constraint violation when validating a bean.

The value of the default message can be hard coded, but it is recommended to use a resource bundle key to allow internationalization. By convention, the resource bundle key should be the fully qualified class name of the constraint annotation concatenated to .message.

```
// Hard coded error message
String message() default "Invalid ISBN number";
// Resource bundle key
String message() default "{org.agoncal.fascicle.Isbn.message}";
```

6.4.1. Templates

Thanks to message interpolation (javax.validation.MessageInterpolator interface), the error message can contain placeholders. The goal of interpolation is to determine the error message by resolving the message strings and the parameters between braces. The error message that follows is interpolated so the {value} placeholder is replaced by the value of the corresponding elements:

```
org.agoncal.fascicle.Isbn.message = {value} is an invalid ISBN number
```

As seen in Chapter 4, you can use resource bundles to internationalize your own error messages.

6.5. Class-level Constraints

So far, you've seen different ways of developing a constraint that is applied to an attribute (or a getter), a method/constructor parameter, and returned value. But you can also create a constraint for an entire bean. The idea is to express a constraint which is based on several properties of a given class.

Listing 54 shows a purchase order class. This purchase order follows a certain business life cycle: it is created into the system, paid by the customer, and then delivered to the customer. This class keeps track of all these events by having a corresponding creationDate, paymentDate, and deliveryDate. The class-level annotation (or class-level constraint) @ChronologicalDates is there to check that these three dates are in chronological order.

Listing 54. A Class-Level Constraint Checking Chronological Dates

```
@ChronologicalDates
public class Order {

    private LocalDate creationDate;
    private LocalDate paymentDate;
    private LocalDate deliveryDate;
    private Double totalAmount;
    private List<OrderLine> orderLines;

    // Constructors, getters, setters
}
```

Listing 55 shows the implementation of the @ChronologicalDates constraint. Like the constraints you've seen so far, it implements the ConstraintValidator interface whose generic type is Order. The isValid() method checks that the three dates are in chronological order and returns true if they are.

Listing 55. The ChronologicalDates Class-level Constraint Implementation

```
public class ChronologicalDatesValidator implements ConstraintValidator
<ChronologicalDates, Order> {

  @Override
  public boolean isValid(Order order, ConstraintValidatorContext ctx) {
    if (order.getCreationDate()==null || order.getDeliveryDate() == null || order
.getPaymentDate() == null)
      return true;

    return order.getCreationDate().isBefore(order.getPaymentDate()) &&
          order.getPaymentDate().isBefore(order.getDeliveryDate());
  }
}
```

In Listing 55, @ChronologicalDates is a class-level constraint which is based on several properties of the Order class (in this case it makes sure that the creationDate, paymentDate, and deliveryDate are all chronological). The way to validate such a constraint is as usual. In the code below, we set the correct chronological dates to the Order object and validate it. Being valid, the size of the set of ConstraintViolation is zero.

```
Order order = new Order();
order.setCreationDate(LocalDate.parse("2018-01-10"));
order.setPaymentDate(LocalDate.parse("2018-01-20"));
order.setDeliveryDate(LocalDate.parse("2018-01-30"));

Set<ConstraintViolation<Order>> violations = validator.validate(order);
assertEquals(0, violations.size());
```

On the other hand, if we enter random dates (which are not chronological), the bean becomes invalid and the size of ConstraintViolation set will be one.

```
Order order = new Order();
order.setCreationDate(LocalDate.parse("2018-01-30"));
order.setPaymentDate(LocalDate.parse("2018-01-20"));
order.setDeliveryDate(LocalDate.parse("2018-01-10"));

Set<ConstraintViolation<Order>> violations = validator.validate(order);
assertEquals(1, violations.size());
```

Class-level constraints are a good way to move the validation logic out of your business code, ending up with clean business code. Also, if the validation rules change, you just modify the validator class instead of your business code.

[47] Hibernate Validator additional constraints http://beanvalidation.org/resources

Chapter 7. Advanced Topics

Bean Validation is a very easy-to-use technology. With a few APIs, you can validate beans, use built-in constraints or create your own ones. With a few lines of code, you can check for the constraint violations, display error messages, internationalize error messages and so on. The previous chapters have shown you the power and the simplicity of Bean Validation. But sometimes you might want to go further and dig into less common validation use cases. This chapter explains a few corner cases that you might use from time to time.

The code in this chapter can be found at https://github.com/agoncal/agoncal-fascicle-bean-validation/tree/2.0/advanced

7.1. Constraint Inheritance

Often a business model has inheritance. And with Bean Validation you end up with constraints on your business model classes, superclasses, or interfaces. Constraint inheritance on properties works like normal inheritance in Java: it is cumulative. This means that when a bean inherits from another, its constraints are also inherited and will be validated.

Listing 57 shows the CD class that extends from Item (Listing 56). Both have attributes with some constraints on them. If an instance of CD is validated, not only its constraints are validated but also the constraint from the parent class.

Listing 56. An Item Superclass Using Constraints

```java
public class Item {

    @NotNull
    protected Long id;
    @NotNull @Size(min = 4, max = 50)
    protected String title;
    protected Float price;
    protected String description;

    @NotNull
    public Float calculateVAT() {
        return price * 0.196f;
    }

    @NotNull
    public Float calculatePrice(@DecimalMin("1.2") Float rate) {
        return price * rate;
    }
}
```

Listing 57. A CD Class Extending Item

```
public class CD extends Item {

    @Pattern(regexp = "[A-Z][a-z]+")
    private String musicCompany;
    @Max(value = 5)
    private Integer numberOfCDs;
    private Float totalDuration;
    @MusicGenre
    private String genre;

    // ConstraintDeclarationException: not allowed when method overriding
    // public Float calculatePrice(@DecimalMin("1.4") Float rate) {
    //    return price * rate;
    // }
}
```

The same inheritance mechanism applies to method-level constraints. The `calculateVAT()` method declared in `Item` is inherited by `CD` and `@NotNull` constraint is validated whether the method is called on a `CD` or an `Item` instance. But in the case of method overriding, special care must be taken when defining parameter constraints. Only the root overridden method can be annotated with parameter constraints and not the overriding method(s). The reason for this restriction is that the preconditions must not be strengthened in subtypes. Conversely, return value constraints may be added in subtypes without any restrictions (you can strengthen the postconditions).

If we uncomment the `calculatePrice()` method in the CD class (see Listing 57), the Bean Validation runtime will throw a `javax.validation.ConstraintDeclarationException` saying that a method overriding another method must not redefine the parameter constraint configuration.

7.2. Groups

In the previous chapter, we saw that, when creating a new constraint, the constraint annotation has to define a `groups` element.

```
Class<?>[] groups() default {};
```

So far, we have validated the entire set of constraints for a bean. Groups allow us to restrict the set of constraints applied during validation.

7.2.1. Grouping Constraints

When a bean is validated it means that all the constraints are validated once at the same time. But what if you need to partially validate your bean (a subset of constraints) or to control the order in which constraints are evaluated? For example, you have constraints that are easy to check and constraints that are pretty heavy: you define two groups and validate the easy ones first. That's when groups and group sequences come into play. Groups allow you to restrict the set of constraints applied during validation, and sequences provide means for validating constraints in a specific order.

In terms of code, a group is just an empty interface.

```
public interface Payment {}
```

In terms of business logic, a group has a meaning. For example, in a workflow, "Payment" would suggest that the attributes belonging to this group will be validated during the payment phase of the purchase order. To apply this group to a set of constraints, you just need to use the groups attribute to pass the interface to your constraints.

```
@Past(groups = Payment.class)
private LocalDate paymentDate;
```

You can have as many groups as your business logic needs and you can apply multiple groups to a constraint as the groups attribute allows an array of groups.

```
@Past(groups = {Payment.class, Delivery.class})
private LocalDate deliveryDate;
```

Every constraint annotation must define a groups element. If no group is specified, then the default javax.validation.groups.Default group is considered as declared. So, the following constraints are equivalent and both are part of the Default group (@NotNull has no group, therefore, it belongs to the default group):

```
@NotNull
private Long id;
@Past(groups = Default.class)
private LocalDate creationDate;
```

Let's consider the previous use case we saw earlier with the @ChronologicalDates constraint and apply some groups to it. The Order class in Listing 58 has several dates to keep track of the purchase order workflow: creationDate, paymentDate, and deliveryDate.

Listing 58. A Class Using Several Groups

```
@ChronologicalDates(groups = Delivery.class)
public class Order {

  @NotNull
  private Long id;
  private Double totalAmount;
  @NotNull @Past
  private LocalDate creationDate;
  @NotNull(groups = Payment.class) @Past(groups = Payment.class)
  private LocalDate paymentDate;
  @NotNull(groups = Delivery.class) @Future(groups = Delivery.class)
  private LocalDate deliveryDate;
  private List<OrderLine> orderLines;

  // Constructors, getters, setters
}
```

When you first create a purchase order, the creationDate attribute is set but not the paymentDate and deliveryDate. You want to validate these two last dates later in a different workflow phase, but not at the same time as the creationDate. By applying groups you can validate the creationDate in the default group (since no group is specified for this annotation its default group is javax.validation.groups.Default), the paymentDate during the Payment phase, and deliveryDate and @ChronologicalDates during the Delivery phase. Moreover, you can validate the entire bean during the delivery phase with groups set to Delivery on @ChronologicalDates constraint.

As you'll soon see, during the validation, you just need to explicitly mention which group(s) you want to validate and the Bean Validation provider will do the partial validation.

7.2.2. Validating Groups

Groups help us to validate only a subset of constraints (on a given bean) instead of validating all of them. Each constraint declaration defines the list of groups it belongs to. If no group is explicitly declared, then the constraint belongs to the Default group. On the other hand, from the validation point of view, the validation methods have a varargs parameter which can be used to specify which validation group(s) shall be considered when performing the validation. If the parameter is not specified, the default validation group (javax.validation.groups.Default) will be considered. If a group other than Default is specified, then Default is not validated.

In Listing 58, all the purchase order dates are supposed to be @NotNull. So, without the notion of groups, we would have to set all the dates for a purchase order to be valid (not null). In Listing 59, we only set the creationDate, leave the others null, and validate the bean. Validation occurs for the default group only. Therefore, the purchase order is valid.

Listing 59. Validating Default Group Implicitly

```
Order order = new Order().id(1234L).totalAmount(1234.5);

order.setCreationDate(LocalDate.parse("2017-01-10"));
order.setPaymentDate(null);
order.setDeliveryDate(null);

Set<ConstraintViolation<Order>> violations = validator.validate(order);
assertEquals(0, violations.size());
```

The code in Listing 59 implicitly uses the Default group during validation, but it can be explicitly specified like the code in Listing 60. So, the following code is identical:

Listing 60. Validating Default Group Explicitly

```
Order order = new Order().id(1234L).totalAmount(1234.5);

order.setCreationDate(LocalDate.parse("2017-01-10"));
order.setPaymentDate(null);
order.setDeliveryDate(null);

Set<ConstraintViolation<Order>> violations = validator.validate(order, Default.class);
assertEquals(0, violations.size());
```

Now if we validate the same Order bean for the Payment group, then the code in Listing 61 will violate the constraint @NotNull on paymentDate.

Listing 61. Failing on Validating Payment Group

```
Order order = new Order().id(1234L).totalAmount(1234.5);

order.setCreationDate(LocalDate.parse("2017-01-10"));
order.setPaymentDate(null);
order.setDeliveryDate(null);

Set<ConstraintViolation<Order>> violations = validator.validate(order, Payment.class);
assertEquals(1, violations.size());
```

In Listing 62 we just have to set the paymentDate and deliveryDate in the future (remember the @ChronologicalDates(groups = Delivery.class)) and we finally get a valid bean.

Listing 62. Validating Delivery Group with Chronological Dates

```
Order order = new Order().id(1234L).totalAmount(1234.5);

order.setCreationDate(LocalDate.parse("2017-01-10"));
order.setPaymentDate(LocalDate.parse("2017-01-20"));
order.setDeliveryDate(LocalDate.now().plusDays(1));

Set<ConstraintViolation<Order>> violations = validator.validate(order, Delivery.class
);
assertEquals(0, violations.size());
```

Even if all the dates are set (i.e. @NotNull) some to the past (@Past) or to the future, the code in Listing 63 raises a constraint violation: the three dates are all set, but not ordered chronologically (@ChronologicalDates).

Listing 63. Validating Delivery Group with No Chronological Dates

```
Order order = new Order().id(1234L).totalAmount(1234.5);

order.setCreationDate(LocalDate.parse("2017-01-30"));
order.setPaymentDate(LocalDate.parse("2017-01-20"));
order.setDeliveryDate(LocalDate.now().plusDays(1));

Set<ConstraintViolation<Order>> violations = validator.validate(order, Delivery.class
);
assertEquals(1, violations.size());
```

Chapter 8. Integrating Bean Validation with Other Technologies

As you've seen in the previous chapters, Bean Validation can be used as a stand-alone technology. Just embed the needed dependencies in your code, add constraint annotations on your beans, and validate them with the `javax.validation.ValidatorFactory` and `javax.validation.Validator` APIs. But one beauty of Bean Validation is its flexibility and adaptability: it integrates well with other technologies such as JPA, JSF, JAX-RS, CDI or Spring, for example.

 The code in this chapter can be found at https://github.com/agoncal/agoncal-fascicle-bean-validation/tree/2.0/integrating

8.1. Java Persistence API Integration

Java Persistence API (JPA) is a Java specification that manages objects stored in a relational database.[48] JPA gives the developer an object-oriented view in order to transparently use entities instead of tables. It also comes with a query language (*Java Persistence Query Language*, or JPQL), allowing complex queries over objects.

 If you like the format of this fascicle and are interested in Java Persistence API, check out the references for my *Understanding JPA 2.2* fascicle in Appendix E.

Bean Validation has several hooks into Java EE. One of them is its integration with JPA and the entity life cycle. JPA entities may include Bean Validation constraints and be automatically validated. In fact, validation is performed automatically as JPA delegates entity validation to Bean Validation before insert or update. Of course, validation can still be achieved manually, by calling the `validate()` method of a `Validator` on an entity if needed.

Listing 64 shows a `Book` entity with a few Bean Validation constraints (`@NotNull`, `@Digits`, `@Size` etc.). Notice how we can mix JPA annotations (`@Entity`, `@Id` and `@GeneratedValue`) with Bean Validation annotations.

Listing 64. Book Entity with Bean Validation Constraints

```java
@Entity
public class Book {

  @Id @GeneratedValue
  private Long id;
  @NotNull
  private String title;
  @Digits(integer = 4, fraction = 2)
  private Float price;
  @Size(max = 2000)
  private String description;
  @Size(min=10, max = 13)
  private String isbn;
  @Positive
  private Integer nbOfPages;


  // Constructors, getters, setters
}
```

In Listing 65 the `title` attribute of the book is null and we persist this `Book` entity (by invoking `EntityManager.persist()`) to the database. Without any need to programmatically use the `Validator` API, the JPA runtime automatically invokes Bean Validation before persisting the entity. Bean Validation will return a `Set` of `ConstraintViolation` and then, the JPA integration will throw a `ConstraintViolationException` rolling back the transaction. As the result, no data will be inserted into the database.

Listing 65. Rollbacking Transaction When a Constraint Is Violated

```java
EntityManagerFactory emf = Persistence.createEntityManagerFactory("beanvalidationPU");
EntityManager em = emf.createEntityManager();
EntityTransaction tx = em.getTransaction();

Book book = new Book().title(null).price(12.5F).isbn("1-84023-742-2").nbOfPages(354);
assertThrows(RollbackException.class, () -> {
  tx.begin();
  em.persist(book);
  tx.commit();
});
```

JPA entities have a specific life cycle (*Persist, Update, Remove, Load*) and Bean Validation hooks automatically on this life cycle. Data needs to be valid before persisting or updating an entity from the database.

Another interesting integration with Bean Validation is the understanding of some constraints by JPA while generating the database schema. JPA introspects the entities and is able to generate, create and drop database scripts. If JPA finds a Bean Validation constraint that it understands, it can generate the equivalent SQL. As you can see in Listing 66, `@NotNull` gives a `not null` in SQL, and

@Size(max) has an impact on the size of the varchar. Of course, if the validation is too complex or doesn't have any equivalent in SQL (such as @Positive), it is ignored during the script generation.

Listing 66. Create Table Script with Constraints

```
create table Book (
    id bigint not null,
    title varchar(255) not null,
    price float,
    description varchar(2000),
    isbn varchar(13),
    nbOfPages integer,
    primary key (id));
```

8.2. Java ServerFaces Integration

JavaServer Faces (JSF) is a Java EE specification for building component-based user interfaces for web applications.[49] Inspired by the Swing component model and other GUI (graphical user interface) frameworks, JSF allows developers to think in terms of components, events, backing beans, and their interactions, instead of requests, responses, and markup language. Under the hood, the architecture allows you to plug in any page declaration language and render it for different devices (web browser, mobile devices, tablets etc.).

Let's say we want to create a web page to login: we need two text fields (username and password), a button to log in, and some validations of course (is the password long enough etc.). JSF is perfect for this kind of use case. JSF comes with two parts: the JSF page, or the visual user interface (see Listing 68) and the logic that is bound to that page (i.e. a backing bean, see Listing 67). For the validation, same as with JPA, JSF will delegate the validation to the Bean Validation runtime automatically. No need to explicitly invoke the Validator API.

Listing 67 shows what a JSF backing bean looks like. It is a Java class annotated with @Named and @RequestScoped. The @Named qualifier allows us to access the Credentials bean through its name (which by default is the class name in camel case with the first letter in lowercase). That's how, in Listing 68, the JSF page can bind a property (value="#{credentials.username}") or invoke a method (action="#{credentials.login}"). The @RequestScoped corresponds to a single HTTP request invocation. The Credentials backing bean will then be created for the duration of the method invocation and is discarded when the method ends.

Listing 67. JSF Backing Bean with Bean Validation Constraints

```java
@Named
@RequestScoped
public class Credentials {

  @NotNull @Email
  private String username;

  @NotNull @Size(min = 8, max = 20)
  private String password;

  public String login() {
    // Check user
    return null;
  }
}
```

Listing 68 represents the graphical interface. It is a form to let the user enter a username, a password, and press a button. As you can see in Listing 67, the Credentials backing bean has two attributes (username and password) and both have Bean Validation constraints. This means that if the user enters an invalid username, and presses the Login button, the Bean Validation runtime will validate the attributes before invoking the method loggingIn().

Listing 68. JSF Backing Bean

```
<h:form>
  <f:validateBean disabled="false">
    <h:panelGroup>

      <h:panelGrid columns="3">
        <h:outputLabel for="credentialsLogin" value="Username:"/>
        <h:panelGroup>
          <h:inputText id="credentialsLogin" value="#{credentials.username}"/>
          <h:message for="credentialsLogin" styleClass="error"/>
        </h:panelGroup>
        <h:outputText/>
        <h:outputLabel for="credentialsPassword" value="Password:"/>
        <h:panelGroup>
          <h:inputText id="credentialsPassword" value="#{credentials.password}"/>
          <h:message for="credentialsPassword" styleClass="error"/>
        </h:panelGroup>
        <h:outputText/>
      </h:panelGrid>
      <h:panelGroup>
        <h:commandLink value="Login" action="#{credentials.login}"/>
      </h:panelGroup>
    </h:panelGroup>
  </f:validateBean>
</h:form>
```

JSF backing beans can have different life cycles depending on their scope (*Request, Session, Application, Conversation*). Bean Validation automatically hooks on these scopes and validates the backing bean attributes.

8.3. JAX-RS Integration

Java API for RESTful Web Services (JAX-RS) is a specification that provides support for creating web services according to the Representational State Transfer (REST) architectural style.[50] JAX-RS provides a set of annotations and classes/interfaces to simplify the development and deployment of REST endpoints. It also brings a client API to programmatically invoke REST endpoints.

Let's say we have a REST endpoint to create a new author. Listing 69 shows this Author bean.

Listing 69. Author Bean with Validation Constraints

```java
public class Author {

  @NotNull
  private Long id;
  @NotNull @Size(min = 2, max = 50)
  private String firstName;
  @NotNull
  private String lastName;
  @Size(max = 2000)
  private String bio;
  @Email
  private String email;

  // Constructors, getters, setters
}
```

JAX-RS is a very elegant API allowing you to describe a RESTful web service with only a few annotations. RESTful web services are POJOs that have at least one method annotated with @javax.ws.rs.Path and an HTTP method annotation (e.g @GET, @POST, etc.). The AuthorEndpoint in Listing 70 is a Java class annotated with @Path, indicating that the resource will be hosted at the URI path /authors. The createAuthor() method is marked to process HTTP POST requests (using the @POST annotation) and consumes JSON. To access this resource, you need an HTTP client such as a browser or cURL to point to the URL http://localhost:8080/authors.

The createAuthor() method in Listing 70 takes a JSON representation of an Author and stores it into a persistent store. This method is invoked with an HTTP POST request and returns a Response with the URI of the new author (e.g. http://localhost:8080/authors/1234) as well as the created status (201 Created). But we need to validate the data that gets into the createAuthor() method. Using the @javax.validation.Valid annotation, JAX-RS will delegate the validation to the Bean Validation provider which will make sure the Author parameter is valid.

Listing 70. JAX-RS Endpoint with Constraint Parameters

```java
@Path("/authors")
public class AuthorEndpoint {

  @POST
  @Consumes("application/json")
  public Response createAuthor(@Valid Author author) {
    // Stores the author
    return Response.created(UriBuilder.fromResource(AuthorEndpoint.class)
      .path(String.valueOf(author.getId())).build()).build();
  }
}
```

To see this validation in action, we can use cURL (or any other HTTP client) and pass a valid JSON. With the command below, we will get a 201 Created, meaning that everything went well and the resource got created.

```
$ curl -H "Content-Type: application/json" -X POST
-d '{"id":1,"firstname":"Douglas","surname":"Adams","email":"douglas.adams@h2g2.com"}'
http://localhost:8080/authors
```

On the other hand, if we post an invalid representation of an author, a 400 Bad Request will get returned. In the cURL command below, the id and the firstname are missing.

```
$ curl -H "Content-Type: application/json" -X POST
-d '{"surname":"Adams","email":"douglas.adams@h2g2.com"}'
http://localhost:8080/authors
```

As you can see in this example, validation is transparent, and JAX-RS takes care of returning the right HTTP code (either 200 or 400, depending if there are constraints violatedor not).

 cURL (http://curl.haxx.se/) is a command-line tool for transferring files with URL syntax via protocols such as HTTP, FTP, SFTP, SCP, and many more. You can send HTTP commands, change HTTP headers, and so on.

8.4. CDI Integration

Context and Dependency Injection (CDI) is a central technology in Jakarta EE or in MicroProfile.[51] Its programming model turns nearly every component into an injectable, interceptable and manageable bean. CDI is built on the concept of *"loose coupling, strong typing"*, meaning that beans are loosely coupled, but in a strongly-typed way. Decoupling goes further by bringing interceptors, decorators and events to the entire platform. CDI homogenises scopes among beans, as well as context and life cycle management.

One core feature of CDI is its dependency injection mechanism. Just use the @Inject annotation and you can inject any component into any other. And that's exactly what we can do with the ValidatorFactory or Validator when Bean Validation is used in conjunction with CDI. No need to build the Validator programmatically, we just leave the CDI container to inject the Validator with a single annotation and manage its life cycle.

```
@Inject ValidatorFactory validatorFactory;
@Inject Validator validator;
```

Another interesting aspect of the integration between CDI and Bean Validation, is the automated validation of method constraints on CDI beans. This means that in Listing 71, you don't need to invoke the ExecutableValidator programmatically to check the parameters and the validation is made automatically.

```
public void sendOrder(
            @NotNull String street1,
            @NotNull String city,
            @NotNull @ZipCode String zipcode) {
  // complex logic
}
```

In the previous chapters, we saw how to create our own constraints. Sometimes, the validation algorithm is so complex that we need to use external helper classes. With the CDI integration, Bean Validation can inject any kind of external bean with a simple @Inject annotation.

Let's take the example of the zip code. Listing 72 shows an Address bean. This bean has several attributes using the @NotNull built-in constraint. If you take a closer look at the zipcode attribute, it is annotated with our custom @ZipCode constraint.

Listing 72. Address Bean with Home Made ZipCode Constraint

```
public class Address {

  @NotNull
  private String street1;
  private String street2;
  @NotNull
  private String city;
  private String state;
  @NotNull @ZipCode
  private String zipcode;
  private String country;

  // Constructors, getters, setters
}
```

Like every other constraint, @ZipCode is made up of an annotation, but also of an implementation. As you can see in Listing 73, ZipCodeValidator implements the business logic. This algorithm first checks that the zipcode follows a certain pattern, but then, thanks to the CDI integration, it injects the external bean ZipCodeChecker (not shown here) to check if the zipcode is valid or not (checker.isZipCodeValid(value)).

Listing 73. ZipCodeValidator Using CDI Injection

```java
public class ZipCodeValidator implements ConstraintValidator<ZipCode, String> {

    @Inject
    private ZipCodeChecker checker;

    private Pattern zipPattern = Pattern.compile("\\d{5}(-\\d{5})?");

    @Override
    public boolean isValid(String value, ConstraintValidatorContext context) {
        if (value == null)
            return true;

        Matcher m = zipPattern.matcher(value);
        if (!m.matches())
            return false;
        return checker.isZipCodeValid(value);
    }
}
```

CDI is a very rich specification which I won't cover here. The integration between CDI and Bean Validation allows using qualifiers, alternatives, vetoes and so on. Therefore, you could create a very complex constraint relying on these two technologies.

8.5. Spring Integration

The *Spring Framework* was created back in 2003 as an application framework and a container (based on the *Inversion of Control* principle) for Java platform.[52] The framework's core features could be used by any Java application and could be extended for building web applications on top of the Java EE platform.

Today, the term *Spring* means different things in different contexts. It can be used to refer to the Spring Framework itself, or other Spring projects that have been built over time such as Spring Boot, Spring MVC, Spring Security, Spring Data, Spring Cloud, Spring Batch, Spring WebFlux etc.

Historically, Spring had its own mechanism to do validation prior to Bean Validation. It was called Spring Validation. But from version 3.0, Spring started to fully support the Bean Validation API. You can integrate Bean Validation in a Spring-based application almost everywhere, especially if you use Spring MVC or Spring Data.

Let's take a different example this time. Let's say we need a REST API to persist some addresses into a relational database. As Spring supports JPA and Bean Validation, the code in Listing 74 will not be a surprise for you: Address is a persistent JPA entity (@Entity, @Id) and is annotated with Bean Validation built-in constraints (@NotNull).

Listing 74. Address JPA Entity

```java
@Entity
public class Address {

    @Id @GeneratedValue
    private Long id;
    @NotNull
    private String street1;
    private String street2;
    @NotNull
    private String city;
    private String state;
    @NotNull
    private String zipcode;
    private String country;

    // Constructors, getters, setters
}
```

Listing 75 defines the REST controller that allows us to persist addresses thanks to a couple of annotations: @RestController is the equivalent of the JAX-RS @Path annotation that we saw in Listing 70, and @PostMapping is equivalent to @POST. These two Spring annotations indicate that the resource will be hosted at the URI path /addresses.

The createAddress() method in Listing 75 receives an Address within the HTTP request (@RequestBody Address) and stores it into a relational database thanks to the addressRepository. This method is invoked with an HTTP POST and returns a ResponseEntity with the URI of the new address (e.g. http://localhost:8080/addresses/1234) as well as the created status (201 Created). Before persisting, we need to validate the address, that's why we use the @Valid annotation. Spring will delegate the validation to the Bean Validation runtime before invoking the createAddress() method.

Listing 75. Spring REST Controller

```java
@RestController
public class AddressEndpoint {

  private final AddressRepository addressRepository;

  public AddressEndpoint(AddressRepository addressRepository) {
    this.addressRepository = addressRepository;
  }

  @PostMapping("/addresses")
  public ResponseEntity<Address> createAddress(@Valid @RequestBody Address address)
throws URISyntaxException {
    Address result = addressRepository.save(address);
    return ResponseEntity.created(new URI("/addresses/" + address.getId())).body
(result);
  }
}
```

Listing 76 shows how we can test such a REST controller with a mockAddressEndpoint (an instance of Spring MockMVC class which acts as the main entry point for server-side Spring MVC testing). We create a valid Address, perform a post on the URL /addresses and expect the status code to be 200 (isCreated()).

Listing 76. Testing the Creation of a Valid Address

```java
Address address = new Address().street1("233 Spring Street").city("New York").state(
"NY").zipcode("12345").country("USA");

mockAddressEndpoint.perform(post("/addresses")
  .contentType("application/json")
  .content(convertObjectToJsonBytes(address)))
  .andExpect(status().isCreated());
```

On the contrary, Listing 77 shows how to test the creation of an invalid address. We basically do the exact same thing, except that we set street1 to null, and expect the status code to be 400 (isBadRequest()).

Listing 77. Testing the Creation of an Invalid Address

```java
Address address = new Address().street1(null).city("New York").state("NY").zipcode(
"12345").country("USA");

mockAddressEndpoint.perform(post("/addresses")
  .contentType("application/json")
  .content(convertObjectToJsonBytes(address)))
  .andExpect(status().isBadRequest());
```

Spring has an amazing support for Bean Validation. In this example, we validated the parameters of a REST controller, but we could have done the same on a transactional service or any other injected Spring bean.

[48] JPA https://jcp.org/en/jsr/detail?id=338

[49] JSF https://www.jcp.org/en/jsr/detail?id=372

[50] JAX-RS https://jcp.org/en/jsr/detail?id=370

[51] CDI https://jcp.org/en/jsr/detail?id=365

[52] Spring https://spring.io

Chapter 9. Putting It All Together

Now that you've read all the previous chapters on Bean Validation, it's time to put some of these concepts all together and write a slightly more complex example. In this chapter, we will write a few Java beans where we can apply built-in constraints as well as developing our own.

The idea is to write a graph of objects (see Figure 8) that represents a purchase order and add few test cases to validate our constraints. You'll then compile it with Maven and run it with Hibernate Validation. To show how easy it is to integration-test a constraint, I will show you how to write a test class (OrderTest) with JUnit 5.x.

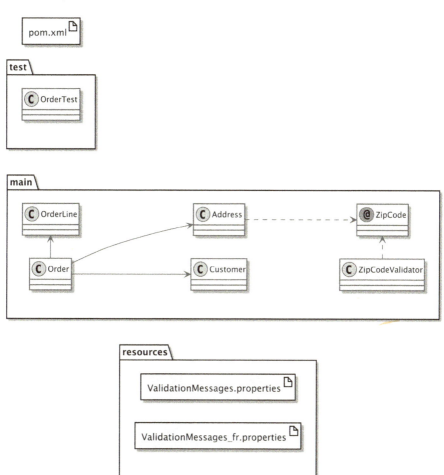

Figure 8. Putting it all together

The classes and files described in Figure 8 follow the Maven directory structure and have to be placed in the following directories:

- src/main/java: The directory for the Order, OrderLine, Customer, Address beans and ZipCode constraint.

- src/main/resources: The `ValidationMessages.properties` and `ValidationMessages_fr.properties` files for the constraints error messages (in English and French).

- src/test/java: The directory for the integration tests `OrderTest`.

- pom.xml: The Maven Project Object Model (POM) describing the project and its dependencies.

 Make sure your development environment is set up to execute the code in this chapter. You can go to Appendix A to check that you have all the required tools installed, in particular JDK 11.0.10 or higher and Maven 3.6.x or higher. The code in this chapter can be found at https://github.com/agoncal/agoncal-fascicle-bean-validation/tree/2.0/putting-together

9.1. Writing the Constraints

The class diagram in Figure 9 represents the domain model for a purchase order. The central class in this diagram is the `Order` which has a set of `OrderLine`. This purchase order also relates to a `Customer` and a delivery address (`Address`). All beans have built-in constraints (`@NotNull`, `@Size`, `@Past` etc.) on their attributes and `Order` uses graph validation (`@Valid`). An `Address` has a zipcode which is constrained through a `@ZipCode` constraint for which we will write a validator.

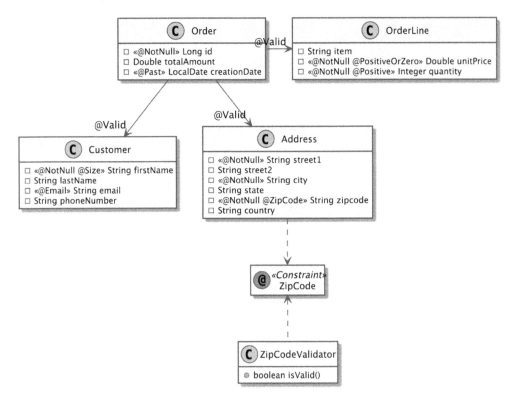

Figure 9. Domain model

9.1.1. Writing the Order and OrderLine Beans

In the Vintage Store application, once a customer has bought a list of items (CDs or books), a purchase order is created. A purchase order (see Listing 78) has an identifier, a total amount and a list of order lines (see Listing 79). Notice that most of the Order attributes are constrained (@NotNull, @Past) but most important, each relation (orderLines, deliveryAddress and customer) uses graph validation (through the @Valid annotation).

Listing 78. Order Bean Cascading Validation

```java
public class Order {

    @NotNull
    private Long id;
    private BigDecimal totalAmount;
    @Past
    private LocalDate creationDate;
    @NotNull @Valid
    private Customer customer;
    @Valid
    private Address deliveryAddress;
    @NotNull
    private List<@Valid OrderLine> orderLines;

    // Constructors, getters, setters
}
```

An Order is made up of several mandatory order lines. Each OrderLine describes the item bought by the customer (CD or book), the unit price, and the quantity the customer has ordered.

Listing 79. OrderLine Using Built-in Constraints

```java
public class OrderLine {

    private String item;
    @NotNull @PositiveOrZero
    private BigDecimal unitPrice;
    @NotNull @Positive
    private Integer quantity;

    // Constructors, getters, setters
}
```

9.1.2. Writing the Customer Bean

Each purchase order belongs to a customer. Listing 80 shows the Customer bean with some built-in constraints on attributes (firstname cannot be null or less than two characters), as well the @Email constraint that checks if the String email is a well-formed email address.

Listing 80. A Customer Bean with Built-in Constraints

```
public class Customer {

  @NotNull @Size(min = 2)
  private String firstName;
  private String lastName;
  @Email
  private String email;
  private String phoneNumber;

  // Constructors, getters, setters
}
```

9.1.3. Writing the Address Bean

An Order has zero or one delivery address. An Address is a bean that has all the needed information for the items to be shipped to the customer: street, city, state, zip code, and country. Listing 81 shows the Address bean with the @NotNull constraint applied on crucial attributes (street1, city, and zipcode) as well as the @ZipCode constraint that checks if a zip code is valid.

Listing 81. An Address Bean with Built-in and @ZipCode Constraints

```
public class Address {

  @NotNull
  private String street1;
  private String street2;
  @NotNull
  private String city;
  private String state;
  @NotNull @ZipCode
  private String zipcode;
  private String country;

  // Constructors, getters, setters
}
```

 Remember that you can download the code from https://github.com/agoncal/agoncal-fascicle-bean-validation/tree/2.0

9.1.4. Writing the @ZipCode Constraint

An Address has a zipcode (in Listing 81) and we need this zipcode to be not null but also to be valid. For that, we need to create our own @ZipCode constraint (see Listing 82). A zip code has a certain format (e.g. five digits in the United States) and this can be checked with a regular expression. The ZipCode constraint annotation in Listing 82 needs an implementation class (ZipCodeValidator in Listing 83). Notice that the error message is a key ({org.agoncal.fascicle.ZipCode.message}) that has to be defined in a resource bundle.

Listing 82. The @ZipCode Constraint Annotation

```
@Constraint(validatedBy = ZipCodeValidator.class)
@Repeatable(ZipCode.List.class)
@Target({METHOD, FIELD, ANNOTATION_TYPE, CONSTRUCTOR, PARAMETER})
@Retention(RUNTIME)
@Documented
public @interface ZipCode {

  String message() default "{org.agoncal.fascicle.ZipCode.message}";
  Class<?>[] groups() default {};
  Class<? extends Payload>[] payload() default {};

  @Target({METHOD, FIELD, ANNOTATION_TYPE, CONSTRUCTOR, PARAMETER})
  @Retention(RUNTIME)
  @Documented
  @interface List {
    ZipCode[] value();
  }
}
```

Listing 83 shows the ZipCode constraint implementation class. ZipCodeValidator implements the javax.validation.ConstraintValidator interface with the generic type String. The isValid() method implements the validation algorithm that consists of matching a regular expression pattern. Notice the null check at the beginning of this method. As explained earlier, it is good practice to consider a null value as valid. If you need a zipcode to be valid and not null, then you would add two different constraints: @ZipCode and @NotNull.

Listing 83. The ZipCodeValidator Constraint Implementation

```
public class ZipCodeValidator implements ConstraintValidator<ZipCode, String> {

  private static final Pattern zipPattern = Pattern.compile("\\d{5}(-\\d{5})?");

  @Override
  public boolean isValid(String value, ConstraintValidatorContext context) {
    if (value == null)
      return true;

    Matcher m = zipPattern.matcher(value);
    if (!m.matches())
      return false;
    return true;
  }
}
```

As you see in Listing 82, the @ZipCode constraint uses a key for the error message (org.agoncal.fascicle.ZipCode.message). This error message is then internationalized in English and

French through property files (see Listing 84).

Listing 84. ZipCode Error Message in English ValidationMessages.properties

```
{org.agoncal.fascicle.ZipCode.message}=invalid zipcode
```

Listing 85. ZipCode Error Message in French ValidationMessages_fr.properties

```
{org.agoncal.fascicle.ZipCode.message}=code postal invalide
```

9.2. Writing the OrderTest Integration Tests

Now, let's test some different scenarios; a scenario with a valid Order containing valid order lines, a valid customer and a valid address, and another scenario showing that the graph validation is taken into account.

Listing 86 shows the OrderTest class that tests the Order bean. The init() method initialises the Validator (using the ValidatorFactory) and the close() method releases the factory.

Listing 86. The OrderTest Integration Test

```
public class OrderTest {

  private static ValidatorFactory vf;
  private static Validator validator;

  @BeforeAll
  static void init() {
    vf = Validation.buildDefaultValidatorFactory();
    validator = vf.getValidator();
  }

  @AfterAll
  static void close() {
    vf.close();
  }

  // ...
```

The class consists of two tests. The first one in Listing 87 creates a valid Order object, with a valid customer, address and two valid orderLines. The code tests that the set of violated constraints is empty, meaning that there are no validation errors and the entire object graph is valid.

Listing 87. Integration Test Succeeding

```
Order order = new Order().id(1234L).totalAmount(BigDecimal.valueOf(40.5)).
creationDate(LocalDate.MIN);
order.setCustomer(new Customer().firstName("Antonio").lastName("Goncalves").email(
"agoncal.fascicle@gmail.com"));
order.setDeliveryAddress(new Address().street1("233 Spring Street").city("New York")
.state("NY").zipcode("12345").country("USA"));
order.add(new OrderLine().item("Help").quantity(1).unitPrice(BigDecimal.valueOf(10.5)
));
order.add(new OrderLine().item("Sergeant Pepper").quantity(2).unitPrice(BigDecimal
.valueOf(15d)));

Set<ConstraintViolation<Order>> violations = validator.validate(order);
assertEquals(0, violations.size());
```

Listing 88 follows the same pattern, except that it sets the customer's firstName to null (violating the @NotNull constraint) as well as a wrong email address. The size of the violated constraints set is equal to two.

Listing 88. Integration Test Failing

```
Order order = new Order().id(1234L).totalAmount(BigDecimal.valueOf((40.5)))
.creationDate(LocalDate.MIN);
order.setCustomer(new Customer().firstName(null).lastName("Goncalves").email(
"wrongEmail"));
order.setDeliveryAddress(null);
order.add(new OrderLine().item("Help").quantity(1).unitPrice(BigDecimal.valueOf(10.5)
));
order.add(new OrderLine().item("Sergeant Pepper").quantity(2).unitPrice(BigDecimal
.valueOf(15d)));

Set<ConstraintViolation<Order>> violations = validator.validate(order);
assertEquals(2, violations.size());
```

9.3. Compiling and Testing with Maven

All the classes now need to be compiled before they get tested. The pom.xml in Listing 89 declares all the necessary dependencies to compile the code: Hibernate Validator 6.x (the reference implementation for Bean Validation 2.0) and the expression language engine.

Listing 89. The pom.xml File to Compile and Test the Code

```xml
<project xmlns:xsi="http://www.w3.org/2001/XMLSchema-instance"
        xmlns="http://maven.apache.org/POM/4.0.0"
        xsi:schemaLocation="http://maven.apache.org/POM/4.0.0
http://maven.apache.org/xsd/maven-4.0.0.xsd">
  <modelVersion>4.0.0</modelVersion>

  <groupId>org.agoncal.fascicle.bean-validation</groupId>
  <artifactId>putting-together</artifactId>
  <version>2.0</version>
  <dependencies>
    <dependency>
      <groupId>org.hibernate.validator</groupId>
      <artifactId>hibernate-validator</artifactId>
      <version>6.2.0.Final</version>
    </dependency>
    <dependency>
      <groupId>org.glassfish</groupId>
      <artifactId>javax.el</artifactId>
      <version>3.0.1-b12</version>
    </dependency>
```

To compile the classes, open a command line in the root directory containing the pom.xml file and enter the following Maven command:

```
$ mvn compile
```

To test our OrderTest class, we need a few extra dependencies in our pom.xml: JUnit and the Maven Surefire plugin (that allow testing).

Listing 90. The pom.xml File Dependencies to Run the Tests

```xml
    <dependency>
      <groupId>org.junit.jupiter</groupId>
      <artifactId>junit-jupiter-engine</artifactId>
      <version>5.7.1</version>
      <scope>test</scope>
    </dependency>
  </dependencies>

  <build>
    <plugins>
      <plugin>
        <groupId>org.apache.maven.plugins</groupId>
        <artifactId>maven-surefire-plugin</artifactId>
        <version>3.0.0-M5</version>
        <configuration>
          <argLine>-Duser.language=en -Duser.country=EN</argLine>
        </configuration>
      </plugin>
    </plugins>
  </build>
</project>
```

Then, to execute the integration tests, it's just a matter of executing the following Maven command:

```
$ mvn test
```

The OrderTest class is then executed, and a Maven report should inform you if the tests pass or not. You should see the BUILD SUCCESS message informing you that the tests were successful.

```
[INFO] Results:
[INFO]
[INFO] Tests run: 6, Failures: 0, Errors: 0, Skipped: 0
[INFO]
[INFO] ------------------------------------------------
[INFO] BUILD SUCCESS
[INFO] ------------------------------------------------
[INFO] Total time:  3.830 s
[INFO] ------------------------------------------------
```

Chapter 10. Summary

Bean Validation has a very comprehensive approach to validation problems. It solves most of the use cases by validating properties or methods in any application layer. If you find that some cases have been ignored or forgotten, the API is flexible enough to be extended to properly fit your needs.

In this fascicle, you saw that a constraint is made up of an annotation and a separate class implementing the validation logic. You can then aggregate these constraints to build new ones or reuse existing ones. Bean Validation comes with already built-in constraints, and you can create your own ones (`@CustomerIdentifier`, `@URL`, `@CreditCard` etc.).

In the first version of the specification, Bean Validation only allowed the validation of beans and attributes. This gave us better Domain-Driven Design, by putting the shallow domain validation in the POJO itself and in this way avoiding the anemic object anti-pattern.[53]

From Bean Validation 1.1, the possibility to validate constructors, method parameters and return value was introduced. This now gives us pre and postconditions validation, something close to design by contract. Bean Validation 2.0 introduced the validation of container elements facilitating validation on collections, maps or sets.

This is the end of the *Understanding Bean Validation 2.0* fascicle. I hope you liked it, learnt a few things, and more importantly, will be able to take this knowledge back to your projects.

Remember that you can find all the code for this fascicle at https://github.com/agoncal/agoncal-fascicle-bean-validation/tree/2.0. If some parts were not clear enough, or if you found something missing, a bug, or you just want to leave a note or suggestion, please use the GitHub issue tracker at https://github.com/agoncal/agoncal-fascicle-bean-validation/issues.

If you liked the format of this fascicle, you might want to read others that I have written. Check out Appendix E for the full list of fascicles.

[53] Anemic Domain Model https://www.martinfowler.com/bliki/AnemicDomainModel.html

Appendix A: Setting up the Development Environment on macOS

This appendix focuses on setting up your development environment so you can do some hands-on work by following the code snippets listed in the previous chapters. This fascicle has lots of code samples, and even has a chapter with a "*Putting It All Together*" section. This section provides a step-by-step example showing how to develop, compile, deploy, execute and test the components. To run these examples, you need to install the required software.

Bear in mind that I run all of these tools on macOS. So, this appendix gives you all of the installation guidelines for the macOS operating system. If your machine runs on Linux or Windows, check online to know how to install the following tools on your platform.

A.1. Homebrew

One of the pre-requisites is that you have *Homebrew* installed. *Homebrew* is a package manager for macOS.[54]

A.1.1. A Brief History of Homebrew

The name *Homebrew* is intended to suggest the idea of building software on the Mac depending on the user's taste. It was written by Max Howell in 2009 in Ruby.[55] On September 2016, Homebrew version 1.0.0 was released. In January 2019, Linuxbrew was merged back into Homebrew, adding beta support for Linux and the Windows Subsystem for Linux to Homebrew's feature set. On February 2, 2019, Homebrew version 2.0.0 was released.

A.1.2. Installing Homebrew on macOS

To install Homebrew, just execute the following command:

```
$ /bin/bash -c "$(curl -fsSL
https://raw.githubusercontent.com/Homebrew/install/master/install.sh)"
```

You also need *Homebrew Cask* which extends Homebrew and brings installation and management of GUI macOS applications.[56] Install it by running:

```
$ brew tap homebrew/cask
```

A.1.3. Checking for Homebrew Installation

Now you should be able to execute a few Homebrew commands:

```
$ brew --version

Homebrew 3.0.4
Homebrew/homebrew-core
Homebrew/homebrew-cask
```

A.1.4. Some Homebrew Commands

- brew commands: Lists the built-in and external commands.

- brew help: Displays help.

- brew doctor: Checks for potential problems.

- brew install: Installs a formula.

- brew uninstall: Uninstalls a formula.

- brew list: Lists all installed formulae.

- brew upgrade: Upgrades outdated casks and formulae.

- brew update: Fetches the newest version of Homebrew.

- brew cask help: Displays Homebrew Cask help.

- brew cask install: Installs a cask.

- brew cask uninstall: Uninstalls a cask.

- brew cask list: Lists installed casks.

- brew cask upgrade: Upgrades all outdated casks (or the specified casks).

A.2. Java 11

Essential for the development and execution of the examples in the fascicle is the *Java Development Kit* (JDK).[57] The JDK includes several tools such as a compiler (javac), a virtual machine, a documentation generator (javadoc), monitoring tools (Visual VM) and so on.[58] The code in this fascicle uses Java 11 (JDK 11.0.10).

A.2.1. Architecture

One design goal of Java is portability, which means that programs written for the Java platform must run similarly on any combination of hardware and operating system with adequate runtime support. This is achieved by compiling the Java language code to an intermediate representation called *bytecode*, instead of directly to a specific machine code. This bytecode is then analysed, interpreted and executed on the *Java Virtual Machine* (JVM).

The *Interpreter* is the one interpreting the bytecode. It does it quickly, but executes slowly. The disadvantage of the interpreter is that, when one method is called multiple times, a new interpretation is required every time. That's when the *Just In Time* (JIT) compiler kicks in. JIT is basically the component that translates the JVM bytecode (generated by your javac command) into machine code which is the language that your underlying execution environment (i.e. your processor) can understand—and all that happens dynamically at runtime! When the JIT finds repeated code, it compiles the bytecode and changes it to native code. This native code will then be used directly for repeated method calls, which improves the performance of the system. This JIT is also called the *Java HotSpot* (a.k.a. Java HotSpot Performance Engine, or HotSpot VM).[59] Then, the *Garbage Collector* will collect and remove unreferenced objects.

A.2.2. A Brief History of Java

James Gosling, Mike Sheridan, and Patrick Naughton initiated the Java language project in June 1991. Java was originally designed for interactive television, but it was too advanced for the digital cable television industry at the time. The language was initially called Oak after an oak tree that stood outside Gosling's office. Later, the project went by the name Green and was finally renamed Java, from Java coffee. Gosling designed Java with a C/C++-style syntax that system and application programmers would find familiar. Sun Microsystems released the first public implementation as Java 1.0 in 1996. Following Oracle Corporation's acquisition of Sun Microsystems in 2009–10, Oracle has described itself as the "*steward of Java technology*" since then.[60]

A.2.3. Installing the JDK on macOS

To install the JDK 11.0.10, go to the official website, select the appropriate platform and language, and download the distribution.[61] For example, on macOS, download the file `jdk-11.0.10_osx-x64_bin.dmg` shown in Figure 10 (you should check out the *Accept License Agreement* check box before hitting the download link to let the download start). If you are not on Mac, the download steps are still pretty similar.

Java SE Development Kit 11.0.8

This software is licensed under the Oracle Technology Network License Agreement for Oracle Java SE

Product / File Description	File Size	Download
Linux Debian Package	148.77 MB	jdk-11.0.8_linux-x64_bin.deb
Linux RPM Package	155.45 MB	jdk-11.0.8_linux-x64_bin.rpm
Linux Compressed Archive	172.66 MB	jdk-11.0.8_linux-x64_bin.tar.gz
macOS Installer	166.84 MB	jdk-11.0.8_osx-x64_bin.dmg
macOS Compressed Archive	167.23 MB	jdk-11.0.8_osx-x64_bin.tar.gz
Solaris SPARC Compressed Archive	186.49 MB	jdk-11.0.8_solaris-sparcv9_bin.tar.gz
Windows x64 Installer	151.73 MB	jdk-11.0.8_windows-x64_bin.exe

Figure 10. Downloading the JDK distribution

Double-click on the file `jdk-11.0.10_osx-x64_bin.dmg`. This will bring up a pop-up screen (see Figure 11), asking you to start the installation.

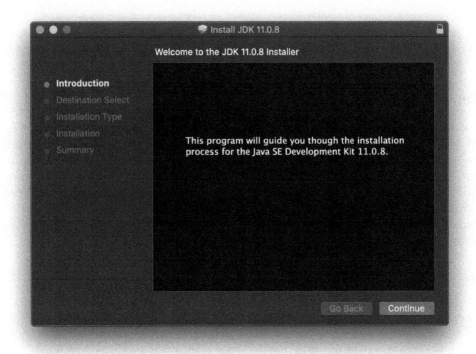

Figure 11. Installation pop-up screen

The wizard invites you to accept the licence for the software and install the JDK successfully (see Figure 12).

Figure 12. Successful JDK installation

There is also an easier way to install Java using Homebrew. First of all, check if you already have the Java formula installed on your machine:

```
$ brew cask list java11
Error: Cask 'java11' is not installed.
```

If the Java formula is not installed, execute the following Homebrew commands to install it:

```
$ brew tap homebrew/cask-versions
$ brew cask install java11
...
java11 was successfully installed!
```

A.2.4. Checking for Java Installation

Once the installation is complete, it is necessary to set the JAVA_HOME variable and the $JAVA_HOME/bin directory to the PATH variable. Check that your system recognises Java by entering java -version as well as the Java compiler with javac -version.

```
$ java -version
java version "11.0.10" 2020-07-14 LTS
Java(TM) SE Runtime Environment 18.9 (build 11.0.10+10-LTS)
Java HotSpot(TM) 64-Bit Server VM 18.9 (build 11.0.10+10-LTS, mixed mode)

$ javac -version
javac 11.0.10
```

A.3. Maven 3.6.x

All the examples of this fascicle are built and tested using Maven.[62] Maven offers a building solution, shared libraries, and a plugin platform for your projects, allowing you to do quality control, documentation, teamwork and so forth. Based on the *"convention over configuration"* principle, Maven brings a standard project description and a number of conventions such as a standard directory structure. With an extensible architecture based on plugins, Maven can offer many different services.

A.3.1. A Brief History of Maven

Maven, created by Jason van Zyl, began as a subproject of Apache Turbine in 2002. In 2003, it was voted on and accepted as a top-level Apache Software Foundation project. In July 2004, Maven's release was the critical first milestone, v1.0. Maven 2 was declared v2.0 in October 2005 after about six months in beta cycles. Maven 3.0 was released in October 2010, being mostly backwards compatible with Maven 2.[63]

A.3.2. Project Descriptor

Maven is based on the fact that a majority of Java projects face similar requirements when building applications. A Maven project needs to follow some standards as well as define specific features in a project descriptor, or *Project Object Model* (POM). The POM is an XML file (pom.xml) placed at the root of the project and contains all the metadata of the project. As shown in Listing 91, the minimum required information to describe the identity of a project is the groupId, the artifactId, the version, and the packaging type.

Listing 91. Header of a Maven Project Descriptor

```xml
<?xml version="1.0" encoding="UTF-8"?>
<project xmlns:xsi="http://www.w3.org/2001/XMLSchema-instance"
         xmlns="http://maven.apache.org/POM/4.0.0"
         xsi:schemaLocation="http://maven.apache.org/POM/4.0.0
http://maven.apache.org/xsd/maven-4.0.0.xsd">

  <modelVersion>4.0.0</modelVersion>
  <groupId>org.agoncal.fascicle</groupId>
  <artifactId>chapter01</artifactId>
  <version>1.0-SNAPSHOT</version>
  <packaging>jar</packaging>
</project>
```

A project is often divided into different artifacts. These artifacts are then grouped under the same groupId (similar to packages in Java) and uniquely identified by the artifactId. Packaging allows Maven to produce each artifact following a standard format (jar, war, ear etc.). Finally, the version allows the identifying of an artifact during its lifetime (version 1.1, 1.2, 1.2.1 etc.). Maven imposes versioning so that a team can manage the life of its project development. Maven also introduces the concept of SNAPSHOT versions (the version number ends with the string -SNAPSHOT) to identify an artifact that is being developed and is not released yet.

The POM defines much more information about your project. Some aspects are purely descriptive (name, description etc.), while others concern the application execution such as the list of external libraries used, and so on. Moreover, the pom.xml defines environmental information to build the project (versioning tool, continuous integration server, artifact repositories), and any other specific process to build your project.

A.3.3. Managing Artifacts

Maven goes beyond building artifacts; it also offers a genuine approach to archive and share these artifacts. Maven uses a local repository on your hard drive (by default in ~/.m2/repository) where it stores all the artifacts that the project's descriptor references. The local repository is filled either by the local developer's artifacts (e.g. myProject-1.1.jar) or by external ones (e.g. javax.annotation-api-1.2.jar) that Maven downloads from remote repositories.

A Maven project can reference a specific artifact including the artifact's dependencies in the POM using groupId, artifactId, version and scope in a declarative way as shown in Listing 92. If necessary, Maven will download them to the local repository from remote repositories. Moreover, using the POM descriptors of these external artifacts, Maven will also download the artifacts they need (so-called *"transitive dependencies"*). Therefore, the development team doesn't have to manually add the project dependencies to the classpath. Maven automatically adds the necessary libraries.

Listing 92. Maven Dependencies

```xml
<dependencies>
  <dependency>
    <groupId>org.eclipse.persistence</groupId>
    <artifactId>javax.persistence</artifactId>
    <version>2.1</version>
    <scope>provided</scope>
  </dependency>
  <dependency>
    <groupId>org.glassfish</groupId>
    <artifactId>javax.ejb</artifactId>
    <version>3.2</version>
    <scope>provided</scope>
  </dependency>
</dependencies>
```

Dependencies may have limited visibility (called scope):

- test: The library is used to compile and run test classes but is not packaged in the produced artifact (e.g. war file).

- provided: The library is provided by the environment (persistence provider, application server etc.) and is only used to compile the code.

- compile: The library is necessary for compilation and execution. Therefore, it will be packaged as part of the produced artifact too.

- runtime: The library is only required for execution but is excluded from the compilation (e.g. Servlets).

A.3.4. Installing Maven on macOS

The examples of this fascicle have been developed with Apache Maven 3.6.x. Once you have installed the JDK 11.0.10, make sure the JAVA_HOME environment variable is set. Then, check if you already have the Maven formula installed on your machine:

```
$ brew list maven
Error: No such keg: /usr/local/Cellar/maven
```

If the Maven formula is not installed, execute the following Homebrew command to install it:

```
$ brew install maven
...
maven was successfully installed!
```

You should now see the Maven formula in Homebrew:

```
$ brew list maven
/usr/local/Cellar/maven/3.6.3_1/bin/mvn
/usr/local/Cellar/maven/3.6.3_1/bin/mvnDebug
/usr/local/Cellar/maven/3.6.3_1/bin/mvnyjp
```

A.3.5. Checking for Maven Installation

Once you've got Maven installed, open a command line and enter mvn -version to validate your installation. Maven should print its version and the JDK version it uses (which is handy as you might have different JDK versions installed on the same machine).

```
$ mvn -version

Apache Maven 3.6.3
Maven home: /usr/local/Cellar/maven/3.6.3_1/libexec
```

Be aware that Maven needs Internet access so it can download plugins and project dependencies from the Maven Central and/or other remote repositories.[64] If you are behind a proxy, see the documentation to configure your settings.

A.3.6. Some Maven Commands

Maven is a command line utility where you can use several parameters and options to build, test or package your code. To get some help on the commands you can type, use the following command:

```
$ mvn --help

usage: mvn [options] [<goal(s)>] [<phase(s)>]
```

Here are some commands that you will be using to run the examples in the fascicle. Each invokes a different phase of the project life cycle (clean, compile, install etc.) and uses the pom.xml to download libraries, customise the compilation, or extend some behaviours using plugins:

- mvn clean: Deletes all generated files (compiled classes, generated code, artifacts etc.).
- mvn compile: Compiles the main Java classes.
- mvn test-compile: Compiles the test classes.
- mvn test: Compiles the main Java classes as well as the test classes and executes the tests.
- mvn package: Compiles, executes the tests and packages the code into an archive (e.g. a war file).
- mvn install: Builds and installs the artifacts in your local repository.
- mvn clean install: Cleans and installs (note that you can add several commands separated by spaces, like mvn clean compile test).

Maven allows you to compile, run, and package the examples of this fascicle. It decouples the fact that you need to write your code (within an IDE) and build it. To develop you need an *Integrated Development Environment* (IDE). I use IntelliJ IDEA from JetBrains, but you can use any IDE you like because this fascicle only relies on Maven and not on specific IntelliJ IDEA features.

A.4. Testing Frameworks

A.4.1. JUnit 5.x

All the examples of this fascicle are tested using JUnit 5.x. JUnit is an open source framework to write and run repeatable tests.[65] JUnit features include: assertions for testing expected results, fixtures for sharing common test data, and runners for running tests.

JUnit is the de facto standard testing library for the Java language, and it stands in a single jar file that you can download from https://junit.org/junit5 (or use Maven dependency management, which we do in this fascicle). The library contains a complete API to help you write your unit tests and execute them. Unit and integration tests help your code to be more robust, bug free, and reliable. Coming up, we will go through the above features with some examples but before that, let's have a quick overview of JUnit's history.

 The code in this appendix can be found at https://github.com/agoncal/agoncal-fascicle-commons/tree/master/junit

A Brief History of JUnit

JUnit was originally written by Erich Gamma and Kent Beck in 1998. It was inspired by Smalltalk's SUnit test framework, also written by Kent Beck. It quickly became one of the most popular frameworks in the Java world. JUnit took an important step in achieving test-driven development (TDD). Let's see some of the JUnit features through a simple example.

Writing Tests

Listing 93 represents a `Customer` POJO. It has some attributes, including a date of birth, constructors, getters and setters. It also provides two utility methods to clear the date of birth and to calculate the age of the customer (`calculateAge()`).

Listing 93. A Customer Class

```java
public class Customer {

    private Long id;
    private String firstName;
    private String lastName;
    private String email;
    private String phoneNumber;
    private LocalDate dateOfBirth;
    private Integer age;

    // Constructors, getters, setters

    public void calculateAge() {
        if (dateOfBirth == null) {
            age = null;
            return;
        }

        age = Period.between(dateOfBirth, LocalDate.now()).getYears();
    }

    public void clear() {
        this.dateOfBirth = null;
    }
}
```

The `calculateAge()` method uses the `dateOfBirth` attribute to set the customer's age. It has some business logic and we want to make sure the algorithm calculates the age accurately. We want to test this business logic. For that, we need a test class with some JUnit test methods and assertions.

Test Class

In JUnit, test classes do not have to extend anything. To be executed as a test case, a JUnit class needs at least one method annotated with `@Test`. If you write a class without at least one `@Test` method, you will get an error when trying to execute it (`java.lang.Exception: No runnable methods`). Listing 94 shows the `CustomerTest` class that initialises the `Customer` object.

Listing 94. A Unit Test Class for Customer

```java
public class CustomerTest {

    private Customer customer = new Customer();
```

Fixtures

Fixtures are methods to initialise and release any common object during tests. JUnit uses `@BeforeEach` and `@AfterEach` annotations to execute code before or after each test. These methods can be given any name (`clearCustomer()` in Listing 95), and you can have multiple methods in one test class. JUnit uses `@BeforeAll` and `@AfterAll` annotations to execute specific code only once, before or after the test suite is executed. These methods must be unique and static. `@BeforeAll` and `@AfterAll` can be very useful if you need to allocate and release expensive resources.

Listing 95. Fixture Executed Before Each Test

```
@BeforeEach
public void clearCustomer() {
    customer.clear();
}
```

Test Methods

A test method must use the `@Test` annotation, return `void`, and take no parameters. This is controlled at runtime and throws an exception if not respected. In Listing 96, the test method `ageShouldBeGreaterThanZero` creates a new `Customer` and sets a specific date of birth. Then, using the assertion mechanism of JUnit (explained in the next section), it checks that the calculated age is greater than zero.

Listing 96. Method Testing Age Calculation

```
@Test
public void ageShouldBeGreaterThanZero() {
    customer = new Customer("Rita", "Navalhas", "rnavalhas@gmail.com");
    customer.setDateOfBirth(LocalDate.of(1975, 5, 27));

    customer.calculateAge();

    assertTrue(customer.getAge() >= 0);
}
```

JUnit also allows us to check for exceptions. In Listing 97, we are trying to calculate the age of a null customer object so the call to the `calculateAge()` method should throw a `NullPointerException`. If it does, then the test succeeds. If it doesn't, or if it throws a different type of exception than the one declared, the test fails.

Listing 97. Method Testing Nullity

```
@Test
public void shouldThrowAnExceptionCauseDateOfBirtheIsNull() {

    customer = null;
    assertThrows(NullPointerException.class, () -> {
        customer.calculateAge();
    });
}
```

Listing 98 does not implement the `shouldCalculateOldAge()` method. However, you don't want the test to fail; you just want to ignore it. You can add the `@Disable` annotation next to the `@Test` annotation. JUnit will report the number of disabled tests, along with the number of tests that succeeded and failed. Note that @Disable takes an optional parameter (a String) in case you want to record why a test is being disabled.

Listing 98. Disabling a Method for Testing

```
@Test
@Disabled("Test is not ready yet")
public void shouldCalculateOldAge() {
    // some work to do
}
```

JUnit Assertions

Test cases must assert that objects conform to an expected result, such as in Listing 96 where we assert that the age is greater than zero. For that, JUnit has an Assertions class that contains several methods. In order to use different assertions, you can either use the prefixed syntax (e.g. Assertions.assertEquals()) or import the Assertions class statically. Listing 99 shows a simplified subset of the methods defined in the Assertions class.

Listing 99. Subset of JUnit Assertions

```
public class Assertions {

    void assertTrue(boolean condition) { }
    void assertFalse(boolean condition) { }

    void assertNull(Object actual) { }
    void assertNotNull(Object actual) { }

    void assertEquals(Object expected, Object actual) { }
    void assertNotEquals(Object unexpected, Object actual) { }

    void assertArrayEquals(Object[] expected, Object[] actual) { }
    void assertLinesMatch(List<String> expectedLines, List<String> actualLines) { }

    void assertSame(Object expected, Object actual) { }
    void assertNotSame(Object unexpected, Object actual) { }
    void assertAll(Collection<Executable> executables) { }
    void assertTimeout(Duration timeout, Executable executable) { }

    <T extends Throwable> T assertThrows(Class<T> expectedType, Executable exec) { }
}
```

Executing Tests

JUnit is very well integrated with most IDEs (IntelliJ IDEA, Eclipse, NetBeans etc.). When working with these IDEs, in most cases, JUnit highlights in green to indicate successful tests and in red to indicate failures. Most IDEs also provide facilities to create test classes.

JUnit is also integrated with Maven through the Surefire plugin used during the test phase of the build life cycle.[66] It executes the JUnit test classes of an application and generates reports in XML and text file formats. That's mostly how we will be using JUnit in this fascicle: through Maven. To integrate JUnit in Maven, you just need the JUnit dependency and make sure to declare the Surefire plugin in the pom.xml as shown in Listing 100.

Listing 100. JUnit Dependencies in a Maven pom.xml

```xml
<dependencies>
  <dependency>
    <groupId>org.junit.jupiter</groupId>
    <artifactId>junit-jupiter-engine</artifactId>
    <version>5.6.0</version>
    <scope>test</scope>
  </dependency>
</dependencies>

<build>
  <plugins>
    <plugin>
      <groupId>org.apache.maven.plugins</groupId>
      <artifactId>maven-surefire-plugin</artifactId>
      <version>2.22.2</version>
    </plugin>
  </plugins>
</build>
```

The following Maven command runs the JUnit tests through the Surefire plugin:

```
$ mvn test
```

Then JUnit executes the tests and gives the number of executed tests, the number of failures and the number of disabled tests (through warnings).

```
[INFO] -----------------------
[INFO] Building Commons :: JUnit
[INFO] -----------------------
[INFO]
[INFO] --- maven-compiler-plugin:3.7.0:compile (default-compile)
[INFO]
[INFO] --- maven-surefire-plugin:2.22.2:test (default-test) .
[INFO]
[INFO] ----------
[INFO]  T E S T S
[INFO] ----------
[INFO] Running org.agoncal.fascicle.commons.junit.CustomerTest
[WARNING] Tests run: 3, Failures: 0, Errors: 0, Skipped: 1, Time elapsed: 0.032 s
[INFO]
[INFO] Results:
[INFO]
[WARNING] Tests run: 3, Failures: 0, Errors: 0, Skipped: 1
[INFO]
[INFO] -------------
[INFO] BUILD SUCCESS
[INFO] -------------
[INFO] Total time:  1.824 s
[INFO] Finished at: 2020-03-04T11:51:34+01:00
[INFO] ------------
```

A.5. Git

Git is a free and open source distributed version control system designed for tracking changes in computer files and coordinating work on those files among multiple people.[67] It is primarily used for source code management in software development, but it can be used to keep track of changes in any set of files. Git was created by Linus Torvalds in 2005 for the development of the Linux kernel, with other kernel developers contributing to its initial development.

Git is not really needed to run the samples in this fascicle. Even if the code is hosted on a public Git repository (https://github.com/agoncal/agoncal-fascicle-bean-validation/tree/2.0), you can either download the code as a zip file, or clone the repository. Only if you clone the repository will you need to have Git installed.

A.5.1. A Brief History of Git

Git development began in April 2005, after many developers in the Linux kernel gave up access to BitKeeper, a proprietary source-control management (SCM). Linus Torvalds wanted a distributed system that he could use, like BitKeeper, but none of the available free systems met his needs. So, Linus started the development of Git on 3rd April 2005, announced the project on 6th April and the first merge of multiple branches took place on 18th April. On 29th April, the nascent Git was benchmarked, recording patches to the Linux kernel tree at the rate of 6.7 patches per second.[68]

A.5.2. Installing Git on macOS

On macOS, if you have installed Homebrew, then installing Git is just a matter of a single command. [69] Open your terminal and install Git with the following command:

```
$ brew install git
```

A.5.3. Checking for Git Installation

Once installed, check for Git by running `git --version` in the terminal. It should display the git version:

```
$ git --version
git version 2.30.1
```

A.5.4. Cloning Repository

Once Git is installed, you can clone the code of the repository with a `git clone` on https://github.com/agoncal/agoncal-fascicle-bean-validation.git.

[54] Homebrew https://brew.sh

[55] Homebrew History https://en.wikipedia.org/wiki/Homebrew_(package_manager)#History

[56] Homebrew Cask https://github.com/Homebrew/homebrew-cask

[57] Java http://www.oracle.com/technetwork/java/javase

[58] Visual VM https://visualvm.github.io

[59] The Java HotSpot Performance Engine Architecture https://www.oracle.com/technetwork/java/whitepaper-135217.html

[60] Java History https://en.wikipedia.org/wiki/Java_(programming_language)#History

[61] Java Website http://www.oracle.com/technetwork/java/javase/downloads/index.html

[62] Maven https://maven.apache.org

[63] Maven History https://en.wikipedia.org/wiki/Apache_Maven#History

[64] Maven Central https://search.maven.org

[65] JUnit https://junit.org/junit5

[66] Maven Surefire Plugin https://maven.apache.org/surefire/maven-surefire-plugin

[67] Git https://git-scm.com

[68] History of Git https://en.wikipedia.org/wiki/Git#History

[69] Homebrew https://brew.sh

Appendix B: Bean Validation Specification Versions

B.1. Bean Validation 2.0

Bean Validation 2.0 is described under the JSR 380 and was released in 2017.[70] This major release brings many new features and improves existing ones.[71] The major new features are:

- Adds support for Java SE 8 (the requirement of Java 8 was the motivation behind creating a major version 2.0 instead of a 1.2).

- Validation annotations can be added to containers such as collections (e.g. List<@Positive Integer> positiveNumbers) and java.util.Optional.

- New built-in constraints: @Email, @NotEmpty, @NotBlank, @Positive, @PositiveOrZero, @Negative, @NegativeOrZero, @PastOrPresent and @FutureOrPresent.

- All built-in constraints are marked as @Repeatable.

- Support for java.util.Optional.

- Support for the new date/time data types (JSR 310).[72]

B.2. Bean Validation 1.1

Bean Validation 1.1 was released in 2013 under the JSR 349 and was part of Java EE 7.[73] This minor release brought many new features and improves existing ones. The major new features were:

- Constraints can be applied to the parameters and return values of methods and constructors. Thus, Bean Validation could be used to describe and validate the contract (pre and postconditions) of a given method.

- Constraints could also be applied on constructors.

- There was a new API to obtain metadata information on constraints and constrained objects.

- Integration with Context and Dependency Injection was increased (injection in validators becomes possible and method constraints could be automatically enforced upon method execution of CDI beans).

B.3. Bean Validation 1.0

The very first version (1.0) of Bean Validation was released in 2009 under the JSR 303 for Java EE 6.[74] Despite being the first version, it was inspired by Hibernate Validator which was an already established validation framework from Red Hat.[75]

[70] JSR 380 https://jcp.org/en/jsr/detail?id=380

[71] Changes between Bean Validation 2.0 and 1.1 http://beanvalidation.org/2.0/#changes-between-bean-validation-2-0-and-1-1

[72] JSR 310 https://jcp.org/en/jsr/detail?id=310

[73] JSR 349 https://jcp.org/en/jsr/detail?id=349

[74] JSR 303 https://jcp.org/en/jsr/detail?id=303

[75] **Hibernate Validator** http://hibernate.org/validator

Appendix C: References

- Bean Validation 2.0 (JSR 380) https://jcp.org/en/jsr/detail?id=380
- Bean Validation 1.1 (JSR 349) https://jcp.org/en/jsr/detail?id=349
- Bean Validation 1.0 (JSR 303) https://jcp.org/en/jsr/detail?id=303
- Bean Validation http://beanvalidation.org
- Hibernate Validator http://hibernate.org/validator
- Oval http://oval.sourceforge.net
- BVal http://bval.apache.org

Appendix D: Revisions of the Fascicle

D.1. 2021-05-03

- Structure
  - Fixed an EPUB issue that was breaking part of Chapter 8
  - Fixed EPUB navigation on Listing
  - Chapter references have now the title of the chapter (eg. from *Chapter 3* to *Chapter 3, Getting Started*)
- Content
  - *CDBookStore* renamed to *VintageStore*
  - Separated main Bean Validation annotations and APIs
  - Added the support of `java.util.Optional`
  - Added an appendix on how to install Homebrew
  - Added *Understanding Quarkus 2.x* and *Practising Quarkus 2.x* Appendix E
  - Added online trainings section Appendix E
- Code
  - JDK 8u201 to 11.0.10
  - Hibernate Validator 6.0.x to 6.2.x

D.2. 2019-05-17

- Content
  - Fix typos
  - Use UK English all over (instead of mixed UK and US English)
  - Add Jakarta EE and Eclipse Foundation
  - Add information on deployment descriptors
  - Add a diagram and restructured the Putting It All Together chapter
  - Add appendix about JUnit
  - Add appendix about revision notes of this fascicle
  - Add appendix about other fascicles by the same author
- Code
  - Fix JUnit 5 and Maven Surefire dependency
  - Updating versions (JDK 8u151 to 8u201, Maven 3.5 to 3.6, Spring Boot 2.0.0.M7 to 2.1.1.RELEASE)

D.3. 2018-02-16

- First publication on Amazon Kindle Direct Publishing

Appendix E: Resources by the Same Author

E.1. Fascicles

The *agoncal fascicle* series contains two types of fascicles. The *Understanding* collection is about fascicles that dive into a specific technology, explain it, and show different aspects of it as well as integrating it with other external technologies. On the other hand, the *Practising* collection is all about coding. So you are supposed to already know a little bit of this technology and be ready to code in order to build a specific application. Below the list of fascicles I have written.

E.1.1. Understanding Bean Validation 2.0

Validating data is a common task that Java developers have to do and it is spread throughout all layers (from client to database) of an application. This common practice is time-consuming, error prone, and hard to maintain in the long run. Besides, some of these constraints are so frequently used that they could be considered standard (checking for a null value, size, range, etc.). It would be good to be able to centralise these constraints in one place and share them across layers.

That's when Bean Validation comes into play.

In this fascicle, you will learn Bean Validation and use its different APIs to apply constraints on a bean, validate all sorts of constraints, write your own constraints and a few advanced topics such as integrating Bean Validation with other frameworks (JPA, JAX-RS, CDI, Spring).

You can find two different formats of this fascicle:

- eBook (PDF/EPUB): https://agoncal.teachable.com/p/ebook-understanding-bean-validation
- Paper book: http://amazon.com/Understanding-Bean-Validation-2-0-fascicle/dp/1980399026 (ISBN: 9781980399025)

E.1.2. Understanding JPA 2.2

Applications are made up of business logic, interaction with other systems, user interfaces etc. and data. Most of the data that our applications manipulate have to be stored in datastores, retrieved, processed and analysed. If this datastore is a relational database and you use an object-oriented programming language such as Java, then you might want to use an Object-Relational Mapping tool.

That's when Java Persistence API comes into play.

In this fascicle, you will learn JPA, the standard ORM that maps Java objects to relational databases. You will discover its annotations for mapping entities, as well as the Java Persistence Query Language, entity life cycle and a few advanced topics such as integrating JPA with other frameworks (Bean Validation, JTA, CDI, Spring).

You can find two different formats of this fascicle:

- eBook (PDF/EPUB): https://agoncal.teachable.com/p/ebook-understanding-jpa

- Paper book: https://www.amazon.com/Understanding-JPA-2-2-Persistence-fascicle/dp/1093918977 (ISBN: 9781093918977)

E.1.3. Understanding Quarkus 2.x

Microservices is an architectural style that structures an application as a collection of distributed services. Microservices are certainly appealing but there are many questions that should be asked prior to diving into this architectural style: How do I deal with an unreliable network in a distributed architecture? How do I test my services? How do I monitor them? How do I package and execute them?

That's when Quarkus comes into play.

In this fascicle, you will learn Quarkus but also its ecosystem. You will discover Quarkus internals and how you can use it to build REST and reactive microservices, bind and process JSON or access datastores in a transactional way. With Cloud Native and GraalVM in mind, Quarkus makes packaging and orchestrating your microservices with Docker and Kubernetes easy.

This fascicle has a good mix of theory and practical examples. It is the companion book of *Practising Quarkus 2.x* where you learn how to develop an entire microservice architecture.

You can find two different formats of this fascicle:

- eBook (PDF/EPUB): https://agoncal.teachable.com/p/ebook-understanding-quarkus
- Paper book: (ISBN: 9798689410418)

E.1.4. Practising Quarkus 2.x

Microservices is an architectural style that structures an application as a collection of distributed services. Microservices are certainly appealing but there are many questions that should be asked prior to diving into this architectural style: How do I deal with an unreliable network in a distributed architecture? How do I test my services? How do I monitor them? How do I package and execute them?

That's when Quarkus comes into play.

In this fascicle you will develop an entire microservice application using Quarkus as well as MicroProfile. You will expose REST endpoints using JAX-RS and OpenAPI, customise the JSON output thanks to JSON-B and deal with persistence and transaction with Hibernate ORM with Panache and JTA. Having distributed microservices, you will implement health checks and add some metrics so you can monitor your microservice architecture. Finally, thanks to GraalVM you will build native executables, and package and execute them with Docker.

This fascicle is very practical. It is the companion book of the more theoretical *Understanding Quarkus 2.x* where you'll learn more about Quarkus, MicroProfile, REST and reactive microservices, as well as Cloud Native and GraalVM.

You can find two different formats of this fascicle:

- eBook (PDF/EPUB): https://agoncal.teachable.com/p/ebook-practising-quarkus (PDF and EPUB format
- Paper book: (ISBN: 9798629562115)

E.2. Online Courses

Online courses are a great way to learn a new technology or dive into one that you already know. Below the list of online courses I have created.

E.2.1. Starting With Quarkus

This course is for Java developers who want to discover Quarkus. It's a mixture of slides and code so you can "Understand and Practice" at the same time. This way, you learn the theory, and then put it into practice by developing an application step by step.

In this course you will go through an entire development cycle. After introducing Quarkus, you will make sure your development environment is set up, and you will go from bootstrapping a Quarkus application, to running it as a Docker container.

E.2.2. Building Microservices With Quarkus

This course is for Quarkus developers who want to discover how Quarkus and MicroProfile handle microservices. It's a mixture of slides and code so you can "Understand and Practice" at the same time. This way, you learn the theory, and then put it into practice by developing a microservice architecture step by step.

In this course you will develop two microservices that talk to each other. After introducing Microservices and MicroProfile, you will make sure your development environment is set up, and you will go from bootstrapping two Quarkus microservices, to running them as Docker containers.

E.2.3. Quarkus: Fundamentals (*PluralSight*)

Quarkus is said to be a Supersonic Subatomic Java toolkit. But what does this mean? This course explains what Quarkus is so you can decide if it's suited for your project.[76]

E.2.4. Microservices: The Big Picture (*PluralSight*)

Microservices are quickly being adopted by companies worldwide. This course teaches you the basics of microservice architectures from a 10,000-foot high view.[77]

E.2.5. Java EE: The Big Picture (*PluralSight*)

This course functions as a technical and business overview of Java Enterprise Edition.[78]

E.2.6. Java EE: Getting Started (*PluralSight*)

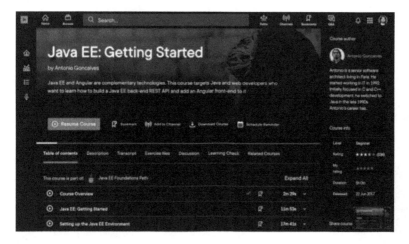

Java EE and Angular are complementary technologies. This course targets Java and web developers who want to learn how to build a Java EE back-end REST API and add an Angular front-end to it.[79]

E.2.7. Java EE 7 Fundamentals (*PluralSight*)

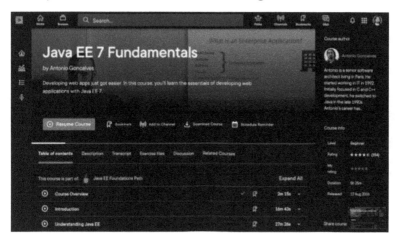

Developing web apps just got easier. In this course, you'll learn the essentials of developing web applications with Java EE 7.[80]

E.2.8. Java Persistence API 2.2 (*PluralSight*)

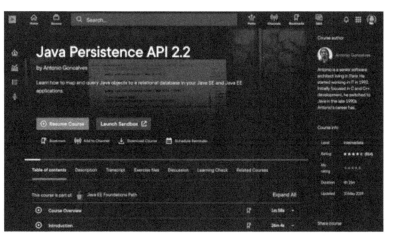

Learn how to map and query Java objects to a relational database in your Java SE and Java EE applications.[81]

E.2.9. Context and Dependency Injection 1.1 (*PluralSight*)

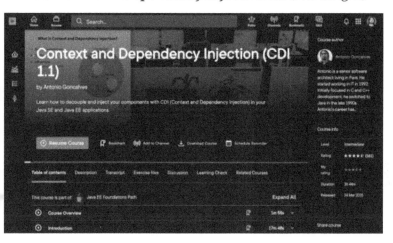

Learn how to decouple and inject your components with CDI (Context and Dependency Injection) in your Java SE and Java EE applications.[82]

E.2.10. Bean Validation 1.1 (*PluralSight*)

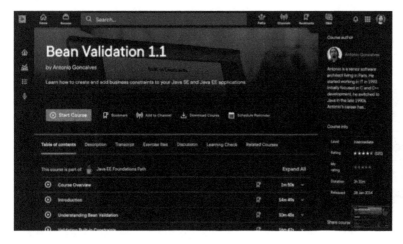

Learn how to create and add business constraints to your Java SE and Java EE applications.[83]

[76] Quarkus: Fundamentals https://app.pluralsight.com/library/courses/quarkus-fundamentals/table-of-contents

[77] Microservices: The Big Picture https://app.pluralsight.com/library/courses/microservices-big-picture/table-of-contents

[78] Java EE: The Big Picture https://app.pluralsight.com/library/courses/java-ee-big-picture/table-of-contents

[79] Java EE: Getting Started https://app.pluralsight.com/library/courses/java-ee-getting-started/table-of-contents

[80] Java EE 7 Fundamentals https://app.pluralsight.com/library/courses/java-ee-7-fundamentals/table-of-contents

[81] Java EE: The Big Picture https://app.pluralsight.com/library/courses/java-persistence-api-21/table-of-contents

[82] Context and Dependency Injection 1.1 https://app.pluralsight.com/library/courses/context-dependency-injection-1-1/table-of-contents

[83] Bean Validation 1.1 https://app.pluralsight.com/library/courses/bean-validation/table-of-contents

Appendix F: Printed Back Cover

Antonio Goncalves is a senior software architect and Java Champion. Having been focused on Java development since the late 1990s, his career has taken him to many different countries and companies. For the last few years, Antonio has given talks at international conferences, mainly on Java, distributed systems and microservices. This fascicle stems from his extensive experience in writing books, blogs and articles.

Validating data is a common task that Java developers have to do and it is spread throughout all layers (from client to database) of an application. This common practice is time-consuming, error prone, and hard to maintain in the long run. Besides, some of these constraints are so frequently used that they could be considered standard (checking for a null value, size, range, etc.). It would be good to be able to centralise these constraints in one place and share them across layers.

That's when Bean Validation comes into play.

In this fascicle, you will learn Bean Validation and use its different APIs to apply constraints on a bean, validate all sorts of constraints, write your own constraints and a few advanced topics such as integrating Bean Validation with other frameworks (JPA, JAX-RS, CDI, Spring).

You can find two different formats of this fascicle:

- eBook (PDF/EPUB): https://agoncal.teachable.com/p/ebook-understanding-bean-validation
- Paper book: http://amazon.com/Understanding-Bean-Validation-2-0-fascicle/dp/1980399026 (ISBN: 9781980399025)

www.ingramcontent.com/pod-product-compliance
Lightning Source LLC
LaVergne TN
LVHW092336060326
832902LV00008B/662